CATHARSIS
IN
LITERATURE

CATHARSIS
IN
LITERATURE

Adnan K. Abdulla

INDIANA UNIVERSITY PRESS

Bloomington

To H. James Jensen
Teacher, friend, and a better critic

Library of Congress Cataloging in Publication Data

Abdulla, Adnan K., 1951–
  Catharsis in literature.

  Bibliography: p.
  Includes index.
  1. Literature—Psychology.   2. Catharsis.
3. Criticism—History.   I. Title.
PN56.P93A23   1985   809'.93353   84-42839
ISBN 0-253-31323-6

1 2 3 4 5   89 88 87 86 85

CONTENTS

CATHARSIS
IN
LITERATURE

Introduction

> There is no hope in returning to a traditional faith after it
> has once been abandoned, since the essential condition
> in the holder of a traditional faith is that he should not
> know he is a traditionalist.
>
> —Al Ghazali

CATHARSIS AS a literary term designating the effects of tragedy on its spectators primarily originates in Aristotle's *Poetics*. The term and its meanings have been a subject of endless controversy through the history of literary theory and aesthetics. Catharsis is a valid and important concept that forces itself into every major critical debate.[1]

The history of literary criticism is not a history governed by abrupt changes, or by the domination of certain literary critics. Rather, it is a history of the contested meanings of basic concepts, such as catharsis, mimesis, and the sublime, or of certain debatable topics, such as the importance of science over literature, reason over imagination, the relation of literature to thought in general, and whether the aim of literature is to please or instruct (and how such pleasure and instruction take place). All these concepts and topics, like chameleons, change their guises in different ages. Some concepts assume new names; some topics come to

the foreground with certain changes in emphasis or focus; other concepts
and topics are relegated to the background.

The debate over catharsis is representative: each age understands it
differently, each major critic gives it certain connotations and understands
it in a way different from other critics. Of all the contested concepts,
catharsis is at least a contestant for the prize of being the most protean.

In classical scholarship, the study of what catharsis means is still
hotly debated, and is still connected to the meanings of Aristotle's phrase
in chapter 6 of the *Poetics* and other uses of catharsis in antiquity. Although the persistence of its use and debate over its meanings indicate
the universality of its application to the function of literature, no systematic study of catharsis in modern criticism exists. Samuel Monk's
pioneering study of the history of the sublime and sublimity is a classic,
and so is Eric Auerbach's study of mimesis, but the study of catharsis
remains scattered in different and multifarious statements in a host of
critics, languages, disciplines, and times. The large amount of data on
catharsis that I have collected lead to two conclusions: first, the discussions of catharsis are not restricted to literary critics, for many
philosophers, anthropologists, psychoanalysts, psychologists, and aestheticians discuss it seriously; second, in each age, because of differing
interests, catharsis acquires a new meaning, a new significance, and new
connotations. Debates over the meaning of catharsis, in short, mirror the
concerns of each age or school of thought. These two realizations (that
there is no definitive study of catharsis and that its meaning changes in
each age) have indicated that to write the history of catharsis would be to
write the history of ideas. The subject is immense, it is complicated, and
it requires great knowledge of different areas of thought.

In my writing on one small corner of the meanings of catharsis, I
encountered a serious difficulty: because of the limitations of time and
space, I had to decide initially what to include and what to exclude in the
discussion of catharsis in modern criticism.[2] To overcome this difficulty, I
have set myself three limitations. First, I restrict my discussion mainly to
literary theory and not to other relevant fields (in the discussion of Freud,
for instance, I concentrate on his thought on catharsis that is strictly
relevant to literary theory, rather than that which relates to psychoanalysis). Second, I restrict my discussion in this study to some important,
representative, modern critics in order to give a general indication of the
modern trends in the meanings of catharsis. Third, I had to limit my
discussion to the main lines of thought and basic modifications that each
prominent critic brings to his discussion of catharsis, omitting other critical interests of the critic in question, and leaving the task of pursuing

catharsis more elaborately in a particular critic or in a particular school of criticism to others who might be interested in studying in detail a single critic or a single school of criticism.

There are three commonly acceptable historical interpretations of catharsis: purgation, purification, and clarification.[3] The first and second interpretations specifically refer to emotions; the third, clarification, refers to intellectual understanding. All three interpretations try to explain the effects of tragedy on its spectators: that is, what happens to us when we apprehend what happens to the hero or protagonist. By extension, the problem can be stated in the following way: what are the effects of art on its readers, and how do these effects come about?[4] The attempt to answer these questions and the narrower question of what catharsis means turn out to be attempts to define the nature and value of literature. Since accounting for the meaning of catharsis involves the broader question of the value of art, the continuing debate on such an important and pervasive subject accounts for the variety of existing discussions about catharsis.

Catharsis is such a complex phenomenon that no one has ever presented a single, definitive statement about what it means, or how it works. Each writer captures only a part of it; each looks at catharsis from his particular point of view, and, by extension, explains it (or, for that matter, the function of literature) from his own ideological or epistemological premises. If such premises are susceptible to changing values, mores, and systems of thought, then it is legitimate to claim that ideas about the meaning and function of catharsis indicate changes in theories and practices of human epistemology, thought, and political systems. Such a hypothesis explains not only why so many thinkers have shown an interest in catharsis, but also the curious fact that the meaning of catharsis changes with author, age, and historical moment. In the Renaissance, catharsis often had heavy moral connotations; in the Augustan age, catharsis was usually thought to be a function of verisimilitude; in the Romantic period, catharsis frequently described the suffering of the poet; in the twentieth century, which is characterized by a multiplicity of critical thought, catharsis has a multiplicity of meanings. Each school of thought manages to wrench out an aspect of catharsis that is appropriate to its own critical focuses or premises. It is no mere coincidence that catharsis, in the last twenty years or so, has acquired an important element: communication. The communicative element of catharsis reflects a basic change, which in turn reflects technological advances in a society that necessitates a new justification for literature, its role in our lives, and its function. Catharsis as communication is a product of our concern with communication, an idea that fits in snugly with the cultural, technological, and scientific climate of the second half of the twentieth century.

The insights of five major thinkers helped me in formulating my own ideas on catharsis: Georg Hegel, Friedrich Nietzsche, Sigmund Freud, Ernst Cassirer, and Georg Lukács. Georg Wilhelm Friedrich Hegel (1770–1831) was the first thinker to make catharsis a universal phenomenon, not one which is merely aesthetic. He did so through what we call the Hegelian Dialectic. It begins with a *thesis* that moves to its opposite, the *antithesis*, by the principle of negativity.[5] The two opposing forces clash, producing a reconciliation of the two, which Hegel calls *synthesis*. Hegel's synthesis, although sharing characteristics of both thesis and antithesis, produces essentially a new state. The Hegelian Dialectic presupposes that all things are related; that nothing exists in isolation; and that everything somehow influences and is being influenced by the forces around it. The Hegelian Dialectic provides us with a fruitful method of understanding catharsis. From the notion of two opposing forces, we can take the classical pity and fear, or good and evil, or attraction and repulsion. The first force (pity, good, attraction) is the thesis; the second force (fear, evil, repulsion) is the antithesis. The clash of the thesis with the antithesis produces a synthesis, a reconciliation, or a catharsis. All this is inherent, but not developed, in the Aristotelian doctrine of catharsis. Explained through the Hegelian Dialectic, catharsis does not simply refer to a literary phenomenon; rather, catharsis is an aspect of the function of art that ultimately is akin to history, life, and the universe. Life is a synthesis of two forces; so is literature; and so is the universe. All are interrelated; none can be explained in isolation. Every force or phenomenon becomes meaningful only if we establish its relatedness and its relationship to the other forces around it. The idea of the Hegelian Dialectic is a major reorienting force in interpreting catharsis that has subsequently influenced every major thinker and critic, including Nietzsche, Cassirer, and Lukács.

Friedrich Wilhelm Nietzsche's (1844–1900) main contribution to catharsis occurs in his first book, *The Birth of Tragedy from the Spirit of Man* (1872).[6] In it, Nietzsche introduces two important terms, *Dionysian* and *Apollonian*. With these terms he distinguishes the primitive side of man from the rational: the Dionysian—which he names after Dionysus, the god of wild flute music, of wine and intoxication, of orgies and festivals—represents the wild, disordered, and unrestrained spirit of man; the Apollonian—which he names after the god of restraint, harmony, and balance—represents in man the spirit of order as it appears in "classical" Greek sculpture and architecture. Tragedy is the product of a tension between these two energies. The impact of the Hegelian Dialectic on

Nietzsche is clear. Nietzsche in 1888 said of *The Birth*, "it smells offensively Hegelian."

Nietzsche argues that for modern man to participate in the experience of a genuine tragedy he must discard his rigid rationality and abstraction. Only after passionate involvement does detachment gain any aesthetic significance. Detachment itself cannot help us understand art; it is, rather, the detachment that follows passionate involvement that gives detachment its importance. Nietzsche considers the birth of tragedy out of the Dionysian cult of music and dances as a triumph for the Apollonia form. He argues that the Greeks faced with the terrors of nature and history did not seek refuge in a "negation of will," but created tragedy, which, despite all the horrors surrounding man, affirms the beauty of life. On an individual plane, the Dionysian aspect of man represents the primitive and the primordial forces in our lives; the Apollonian aspect represents the forces that are rational and harmonious. Both forces coexist in the human mind, but it is only after the recognition of the Dionysian that the Apollonian can triumph. That which is only rational makes us detached, pessimistic, and nihilistic. Indeed, rationality is possible only after we exercise the power to harness irrationality. This is why Nietzsche identifies himself with Dionysus. But Nietzsche's most relevant insights are his emphases on the role of emotions as leading to intellectual understanding, and his contention that rationality (that is, detachment) alone cannot lead to catharsis. Rationality and detachment are meaningful only after we show some emotional involvement in the work of art.

Ernst Cassirer (1874–1945) builds his understanding of catharsis on the foundation of the Hegelian Dialectic, and then expands catharsis in new and innovative ways. After avoiding the confusing entanglement of Aristotelian commentators on the meaning of catharsis, Cassirer affirms:

> What seems to be clear and what is now generally admitted is that the cathartic process described in Aristotle does not mean a purification or a change in the character and quality of the passions themselves but a change in the human soul. By tragic poetry the soul acquires a new attitude toward its emotions. The soul experiences the emotions of pity and fear, but instead of being disturbed and disquieted by them it is brought to a state of rest and peace. At first sight this would seem to be contradiction. For what Aristotle looks upon as the effect of tragedy is a synthesis of two moments which in real life, in our practical existence, exclude each other. The highest intensification of our emotional life is thought of as at the same time giving us a sense of repose.[7]

What Cassirer does in the passage just quoted is of great importance to our understanding of catharsis. First, he rejects the interpretation of catharsis as purification of emotions, an interpretation that has long enjoyed both popularity and prestige among Aristotle's commentators and translators. Second, Cassirer rejects the view of catharsis as inducing change in the character and quality of emotions themselves: in other words, neither pity nor fear are changed nor are they expelled. Cassirer maintains that the change in the reader that occurs during the cathartic process is a change in the reader's soul. Although he does not define what he means by "soul," Cassirer perhaps refers to our intuitive powers that help heighten our perception of art. Admittedly, the soul is a metaphysical quality that defies clear and objective definition, but nevertheless it is a convenient way of explaining the mysterious phenomenon of artistic enjoyment and appreciation, or where the phenomenon takes place.

What is most important in Cassirer's formulations is his affirmation that the cathartic process induces a state of rest and peace to our contradictory emotions. The Hegelian synthesis brings the spectator or reader to a new state, or, as the Greeks put it, a new *stasis*, peculiar to the effect of art on the spectator. In real life, contradictory emotions cancel each other out because of the absence of mimesis. (Mimesis, here, refers to the work of art as an artificial construct, a made thing, where the artist selects and orders his material.) Mimesis in art, because of the selective quality of the events and passions portrayed, eliminates the frills, the confusing details, the elements that in real life blur our vision. In short, the mimetic process intensifies and crystallizes reality in a way that heightens two conflicting emotions: in tragedy we pity the hero or protagonist, but at the same time we are afraid that we might be the target of the same kind of blind forces that lead to the protagonist's downfall.[8] In real life the conflicting emotions stay in a state of constant tension, whereas in art the conflicting emotions are brought to a state of reconciliation, repose, or harmony through the cathartic process. This is why Cassirer says that art intensifies our emotional life, because we exercise our emotions optimally, that is, in the artistic process the work of art directs our emotions toward full expression, which ideally ends in the reconciliation of those emotions. Conversely, in real life, emotions are not reconciled; they stay in a state of tension.

Another original way in which Cassirer looks at catharsis is his assertion that catharsis brings an "aesthetic freedom," where we

> no longer live in the immediate reality of things but in a world of pure sensuous forms. In this world all our feelings undergo a sort of transsubstantiation with respect to their essence and their character. The passions themselves are relieved of their material burden. We feel their form and their life but not their encumbrance. The calmness of the work of art is, paradoxically, a dynamic, not a static calmness. . . . What we feel in art is not a simple or

single emotional quality. it is the dynamic process of life itself—the continuous oscillation between opposite poles, between joy and grief, hope and fear, exultation and despair. To give aesthetic form to our passion is to transform them into a free and active state (p. 148).

There are two basic insights in this passage that are related to catharsis. First is the difference between common, everyday reality, and the reality of artistic experience. The artistic experience lifts us from the mundane concerns of our everyday life into a "world of pure sensuous forms." In this new world of pure sensuous forms, we are detached from the material burdens of emotions, and simultaneously liberated from their encumbrance. The aesthetic experience brings the mind to a new state, a state of dynamic oscillation of opposite feelings.

Cassirer's first insight will be developed and expanded by the Marxist critic Georg Lukács. His second insight is his idea of the feeling of freedom or liberation that follows the elevation of our aesthetic feelings. In the cathartic process, which in this case he associates with comedy, Cassirer maintains, "things and events begin to lose their material weight; scorn is dissolved into laughter, and laughter is liberation." The treatment of catharsis as liberation will be pursued by both Lukács and Jauss; we will investigate Cassirer's second insight in Jauss's writings in chapter 5.

Georg Lukács (1885–1971) in *The Specific Nature of the Aesthetic* (1963) continues the Hegelian tradition of the dialectic inherent in the cathartic process. Lukács bases his four-volume *Aesthetic* on his motion of catharsis, using Hegel only as a starting point.[9] He distinguishes between everyday life (entire man) and the aesthetic moment (man's entirety). Everyday life is heterogenous and pragmatic. Man is a particular being (specific) insofar as he is nonrepeatable and unique, but man is on the level of the human species (generic) only insofar as he speaks, works, eats, etc. Both aspects of our lives (the specific and the generic) are unconscious. It is possible for people to rise from the generic level to the specific level (of the human species) through self-objectification (reification), where a specific "entire man" becomes "man's entirety." In their attempts to rise to the specific level (of the human species), people "suspend" the heterogeneity of the world to become homogenous. In other words, man rises to the specific through the suspension of the generic: man discards his everyday concerns to achieve a unity with others. An individual's rise to the level of "man's entirety" (the specific) makes him identify with the "human cause," and this identification raises (or suspends) him above the mundane concerns of his everyday life (the generic). While on the level of the specific, an individual faces, both consciously and unconsciously, the question of how humane the world is.

That is, he compares his world as he lives in it daily to the world he observes depicted in a work of art. The clash between the generic and the specific (or the homogenous and heterogenous, or the world of the work of art and the real world of the individual) leads to a shock, a shock that Lukács characteristically calls "catharsis." Ágnes Heller comments on Lukács's use of catharsis and says that Lukács makes catharsis

> universal, applicable not just to aesthetics but to the study of entire cultures as well. It becomes a synonymous term for rising to the height of "man's entirety," for the purifying effect of identification with humanity's cause.[10]

In his uses of catharsis, Lukács unites aesthetics with ethics. The aesthetic side of catharsis lies in our "suspension" of everyday life, to rise from the generic, from ordinary human affairs, to the specific, to the aesthetic world of art. The ethical side lies in our contemplation, while we are in the specific, of how humane, how moral our world is.

Sigmund Freud's (1856–1939) impact on catharsis has been more pervasive and far-reaching than any of the other thinkers. I devote the bulk of chapter 2 to his insights. His first insight into catharsis is the necessity of studying identification, a concept that constitutes the first step in the cathartic process. The second insight, probably stemming from Nietzsche's influence, is that the cathartic process begins by emotional arousal (what Nietzsche might call the Dionysian force) and ends with the mastery of a situation (Nietzsche's "Apollonian" force). We feel mastery when we achieve the sense of overcoming the powers of emotions.

Hegel, Nietzsche, Cassirer, Lukács, and Freud provide us with important clues to the understanding in a large sense of what catharsis is, what it implies, and how it functions. Throughout the study I will assume that catharsis presupposes an emotional arousal on the part of the audience. The emotional arousal ends in intellectual understanding or cognition. Cognition could be stated in such simple terms as understanding what is going on in the play, or the drawing of parallels between what we see in the play and our own lives, or even meditating on our conditions as individuals in society and linking that to what we see in the play. Understanding a play, drawing parallels, and meditating on our conditions are different levels of cognition or understanding. Catharsis points clearly to the roles of emotions and of cognition in the aesthetic experience. I shall restrict my vocabulary to the discussion of tragedy, because the elements of tragedy bring into focus the discussion of catharsis in a clearer and sharper way than discussing catharsis in other genres. We begin with the following premises:

A. Catharsis is related to an aesthetic experience and not to everday life experience.[11]
B. In order to experience catharsis the audience must be aware of the conventions and cultural elements of the genre.[12]
C. Catharsis is a culture-bound and a time-bound aesthetic experience.[13]

The three premises allow us to look at catharsis as a process that consists of seven stages. These stages are as follows:

1. Catharsis involves a dialectic: there are two opposing emotions that will give rise to a conflict in the spectator's mind.
2. Such a conflict of opposing emotions requires the identification or involvement of the spectator with the hero of the tragedy, or any other dramatic element in the play.
3. The spectator undergoes an emotional excitation because of his identification with the hero.
4. When the play ends, the emotional excitation is resolved, and the spectator begins to feel repose and serenity.
5. With the resolution of emotional excitation, the spectator begins to draw parallels or comparisons between his life and the hero's.
6. Once the ideation starts (that is, the thinking on the part of the spectator), then the spectator begins to gain an insight into his life, his own affairs, and the humanity of his world.
7. The ideation ends with an understanding of what happened on stage, an understanding that could be moral, metaphysical, or psychological, depending on the spectator's individual character. The spectator feels that he, in Freud's term, is master of the situation.

The seven stages of the aesthetic experience we call catharsis can be reduced to two elements: 1) emotional excitation, 2) intellectual understanding. Put differently, the cathartic response begins with emotive arousal and ends with cognition. The cognitive aspect of the aesthetic experience cannot occur without emotional arousal; indeed, cognition, despite the objections of the Formalists, subsumes emotional involvement.

Here is a more succinct definition of catharsis, which includes the listed steps: catharsis is an aesthetic response which begins with the audience's identification with the protagonist and leads to emotional arousal of two conflicting emotions (e.g. fear and pity). These emotions are resolved by their reconciliation, bringing to the audience a sense of elevated harmony, or peace, or repose, which can be thought of as understanding, whether moral, metaphysical, or psychological.[14] Once we put the mechanism of catharsis into the perspective of stages, we can understand why there are so many interpretations of catharsis. Each different interpretation focuses on one of several aspects of the mechanisms of the cathartic process, but none on all of them. Those who emphasize purgation (expulsion or cleansing of emotions) talk about stage 4, the emotional arousal; similarly, the critics who emphasize intellectual understanding think of the last stages of the cathartic process, perhaps in understanding the effects and causes of the incidents in the play. Emphasis on the cathartic process as stages (rather than concentrating on one part of it) solves another conceptual problem, that of differences in persons and audiences. If a critic refers only to intellectual understanding, he is talking about the last stages in the cathartic process, which in turn assumes a uniform response from all the members of the audience. As individuals and as categories of individuals, we respond differently to the same experience: at one extreme, there is a category of people who enjoy only the emotional excitation; at the other extreme are those who enjoy only intellectual understanding. Since the extremes may rarely, if ever, exist in a pure state, almost all critics emphasize either emotions or intellect. Those who emphasize either extreme, however, go through all the stages of the cathartic process, each lingering on or emphasizing that aspect of catharsis toward which he is influenced by his own personality, personal ideology, and culture.[15]

The interpretation of catharsis and its mechanisms in the stages outlined above helps us understand why catharsis can be interpreted on various grounds. Catharsis can, for example, be interpreted intellectually on moral grounds. Intellectual understanding does not entail abstract thinking about metaphysical problems or categories; by the necessity of being individuals in a society, persons draw parallels between what they see on the stage and their own lives. That is, they learn a lesson from or make whatever use they want of any aesthetic experience they confront. If we take catharsis to indicate the realization of the moral of a play, then catharsis has moral justifications. Intellectual understanding, however, can never occur without some degree of emotional involvement and emotional arousal. We have to become emotionally involved somehow in the action to be able to identify with it. Unless we identify with something externally, the internal excitation that we feel can never occur in the cathartic process. This, too, explains why the interpretation of catharsis only as intellectual understanding is the weakest of all interpretations. It centers only on the last stage of the cathartic process, virtually ignoring the involvement of the reader or spectator in art that precedes and leads to intellectualization.

One of the arguments advanced by some critics to justify the emphasis on the intellectual interpretation of catharsis is Aristotle's frequent references to the idea that learning is pleasurable. What these critics forget is that Aristotle is not talking about an aesthetic experience but about learning in real life situations, learning that could be pleasurable, although what kind of pleasure Aristotle refers to is left to the reader to determine. Learning to fix a chair could be pleasurable, but it is not cathartic. Catharsis is not a simple phenomenon, whether emotional or intellectual. It is a complex aesthetic experience.

There are other contingencies that impose form and method on what I have used in this study. In the argument for the complexity of catharsis and its relevance to modern critical activity, three factors are crucial. First, to study catharsis in one critical school, or worse, in one critic, would give the false impression that interest in catharsis is restricted to an isolated group with an esoteric vocabulary; conversely, to map the diversity and modifications that have occurred in definitions or descriptions of catharsis in the twentieth century, it is necessary to give a critical account of the use of catharsis in several important critical schools or approaches. Second, this study is not a survey of the meanings of catharsis in modern critical thought; rather, it is a highly selective analytical treatment of the way catharsis is discussed or used by prominent twentieth-century critics. Third, in my treatment of individual critics, I have deliberately eliminated differences in vocabulary, critical concerns, and critical focus in order to concentrate on what catharsis means for the prominent critics I discuss, in order to avoid being drawn to their polemics. To avoid the false impression that modern critical activity is consistent and uniform, I provide short introductory remarks both about the critic and the school with which he is associated. The result is a study that, despite its different approaches and names, argues for the relevance and importance of catharsis in modern criticism.

CHAPTER **1** The Historical
Meanings of Catharsis

As to the herd of critics, it is impossible for me to pay
much attention to them, for . . . many of these gentle-
men appear to me to be a sort of tinkers, who, unable to
make pots and pans, set up for menders of them, and,
God knows, often make two holes in patching one.
—SIR WALTER SCOTT

CATHARSIS AS a literary term first appears in Aristotle's *Poetics;* and
so it is important to survey the subsequent layer of meanings with which
Aristotle's use of catharsis has become encrusted before we see how
modern critics use the concept behind it, with or without the use of the
term itself. Critics and commentators have debated the meaning of
catharsis over several millennia, and controversy still goes on. Modern
critics make use of various historical meanings and, more often still, do
not use the term at all because of the ambiguity caused by so much
historical controversy and debate over what it really means. Aristotle,
when he used the term, had clearly hit on a concept important to literature and aesthetics.

Aristotle's *Poetics*, chapter 6, contains the much-debated catharsis
phrase:

Tragedy is, then, an imitation of a noble and complete action, having the
proper magnitude; it employs language that has been artistically enhanced

by each of the kinds of linguistic adornment, applied separately in the various parts of the play; it is presented in dramatic, not narrative form, and achieves, through the representation of pitiable and fearful incidents, the catharsis of such pitiable and fearful incidents.[1]

The term "catharsis" has been translated as "purgation," or "purification," or "clarification," with medical, religious, moral, psychological, or aesthetic connotations, and any critic's particular interpretation of catharsis reflects a frame of reference and priorities. According to Baxter Hathaway,

> Each age, in its attempts to explain what Aristotle meant [by catharsis], has merely mirrored contemporary states of mind. The concept thus has a significance in the history of ideas; it proved a convenient vehicle for diverse aesthetic doctrines.[2]

It is not an exaggeration to say that in the history of aesthetics and criticism no other single concept has created such controversy. Since the Bernardo Segni translation of the *Poetics* into Italian in 1549, its ideas have permeated Western intellectual thought.[3]

One of the most recent statements about catharsis is by Gerald F. Else. Frustrated with varying interpretations of the term, he has recently challenged the traditional status it occupies in both aesthetics and criticism in order to advance his own theory of catharsis. He says:

> We have grown used to feeling . . . that serious literature is hardly respectable unless it performs some "catharsis." "Catharsis" has come, for reasons that are not entirely clear, to be one of the biggest of the big ideas in the field of aesthetics and criticism, the Mt. Everest or Kilimanjaro that looms on all literary horizons. But all this may be nothing but a self-propagating mirage. Aristotle does not tell us that catharsis is so important, that it is the "biggest" idea about tragedy. If it were, we should expect it to be at least mentioned again by name somewhere in the discussion of tragedy. As it is, pity and fear are mentioned repeatedly, and the tragic pleasure three times; catharsis never appears again, by name, after its sudden appearance in chapter six.[4]

His challenge has led to a revival of the old controversy about the meaning of catharsis and how it can be explained either within the framework of Aristotle's philosophy or through its usage in antiquity.

My treatment of catharsis is deliberately exploratory, not only because of the range of interpretations offered by different commentators, but also because of the complexity of the argument and the wide range of the term's possible meanings offered through the ages by critics, commentators, and translators. Although disagreement over the interpretation of the term stems from varying theoretical prejudices and differing aesthetic values held by critics and commentators, we can derive all

exegeses of the meaning of catharsis from one of two sources: the critic
relies on all the contexts in which the term occurs, whether in Hippocrates, Plato, Aristotle, or in other classical writers; or the critic relies
only on the usage of catharsis in the *Poetics*.[5]

I

The first group of historical commentators relies on all the linguistic
uses of catharsis available from ancient Greek. Unfortunately, the term
was not in common use, and it is

> used in a number of unique senses in the extant literature, ranging from the
> medical use of the term to denote a physical purgation, to Socrates' use of the
> word to describe the separation of the soul from the body.[6]

One basic meaning that survives to the modern era derives from ancient
Greek medicine, namely, from a cure associated with the Hippocratic
doctrine of the four humors, a doctrine that presupposed a harmony
between the four humors that kept the body and the mind healthy. It was
thought that one of the factors that disturbed the body's harmonious
balance of humors was the excessive secretion of black bile, which could
be cured by catharsis, the process of driving out the harmful excess by
mystic rites. Participation in those mystic rites "purged" or "cleansed" the
afflicted person from the "pollution." The process made the gods, who
were angry at the person, friendly.[7]

Catharsis could also mean the process of regulating superfluous
quantities of various humors to restore the healthy balance of the bodily
liquids, rather than the entire expulsion of one humor.[8] Catharsis need
not refer to an expulsion of an undesirable fluid, but the process of somehow ameliorating an imbalance of various fluids through music or some
other external force. In other words, both medical meanings of catharsis
have religious connotations because religious rites either regulate the
quantities of emotions or expel the superfluous. Aristotle's use of catharsis
in his *Politics* partakes of both, as he emphasizes the "orgiastic" character
of the flute, and the "ethical" character of other kinds of music.[9] It is
already difficult by now to see which meaning Aristotle intended in his
Poetics.

In dealing with education in *Politics*, Aristotle distinguishes among
three kinds of music: ethical, practical, and enthusiastic. Ethical music
strengthens the mind and the character; practical music has the immediate end of rational education; enthusiastic music is orgiastic or emotional, and its purpose is catharsis. Priests employed enthusiastic music to

cure people who were afflicted by religious mania. In this context, Aristotle makes a statement to the effect that all people experience pity and fear, and religious excitement, but some suffer from an overabundance of them. Priests exposed those who suffered from an excess of enthusiasm to sacred melodies that caused them to become physically excited. Such exciting music left them with calm minds and bodies, as if they were "healed" or "catharated." If we follow Aristotle's argument, then enthusiastic music is neither ethical nor practical in that it neither strengthens the mind nor leads to rational thinking. In other words, enthusiastic music, and its carthartic purpose, is purely emotional, neither moral nor intellectual in its presentation or in its effects.[10]

Aristotle was not alone in making such distinctions. The ancient Greeks generally observed the effects of certain kinds of music on "religious mania" and "enthusiasm." Enthusiasm was thought to be the state induced by the inspiration of a god or other superhuman power that made people frenzied. The Greeks thought that such persons were possessed by a god. In other words, those who were more susceptible to enthusiastic music were vulnerable to the forces of the "dark." Only violent physical dance would, so to speak, shake off the demon and restore peace to the agitated and disturbed mind. Persons were, consequently, referred to priests for treatment, and the treatment was homeopathic. The priests subjected the "enthusiast" to "wild and restless" music to cure him. Catharsis was the name given to the result of such treatment, and the particular kind of music used for treatment was appropriately called "cathartic." According to E. R. Dodds, this particular usage of the term abounds in the writings of the Greeks from Hippocrates to Plato.[11] Dodds also emphasizes the close connection between religious mysteries and purgation:

> If I understand early Dionysiac ritual aright, it social function was essentially cathartic, in the psychological sense: it purged the individual of those infectious irrational impulses which, when damned up, had given rise, as they have in other cultures, to outbreaks of dancing mania and similar manifestations of collective hysteria; it relieved them by providing them with a ritual outlet.[12]

It is not clear from Aristotle's usage of catharsis in the *Poetics* whether he intended the religious or the medical meaning, or even the other meanings that critics and commentators have ascribed to the term. J. Tate says, for instance, that Aristotle's use of catharsis was intentionally ambiguous, since both the religious and the medical contexts come to mean the same thing:

[Catharsis is] the pacification or 'settling' of the (motions arising from the) black bile. He [Aristotle] is making a decided point in calling the religious and the medical effects by the same name. For the only difference between the two is that in the case of the medical purgation there is, in addition to the quelling of pneumatic motions, a literal evacuation. The modern controversy on the question whether the Katharsis of the *Poetics* is to be understood in a religious or a medical sense, is therefore pointless.[13]

What Tate implies is that since the medical sense of the term is figurative (relying on the more physical sense of "motion" as including "emotions"), then the religious sense becomes somehow similar to the medical. But, obviously, the difference between the two senses cannot be brushed aside so easily, because we do not know for sure which usage comes first: the religious or the medical. Hence we do not know which one is figurative and which one is the literal, a question that will determine the origin of catharsis and whether it started in literature or in other disciplines. To complicate matters further, there is also the specific Hippocratic homeopathic medical practice, and later the Aesculapian therapy, where catharsis was the result of a process employed to drive out the detrimental elements in the body (or the mind) by exposing it to an excess of the harmful element. What extinguishes heat is an excess of heat; therefore, they cured fever by exposing a patient to more heat. According to Pottle, "You can alleviate morbid symptoms by a treatment which would produce similar symptoms in a healthy body."[14]

Such an idea historically became associated with literature in the sense that tragedy drives out of the reader or spectator the same kind of emotions presented on stage. The idea had a long history. Milton, for example, in his preface to *Samson Agonistes* (1671) makes the connection between homeopathic medicine and tragedy:

Tragedy, as it was anciently composed, hath been ever held the gravest, moralest, and most profitable of all other poems; therefore said by Aristotle to be of power, by raising pity and fear, or terror, to purge the mind of those and such like emotions; that is to temper or reduce them to just measure with a kind of delight stirred up by reading or seeing those passions well imitated. Nor is Nature herself wanting in her own effects to make good his assertion, for so, in physick, things of melancholick hue and quality are used against melancholy, sour against sour, salt to remove salt humour.[15]

After the Renaissance, the medical metaphor associated with catharsis gradually went into oblivion, and the whole question was not reopened again until 1857, when Jakob Bernays published a pamphlet entitled *Grundzüge der Verloren Abhandlung des Aristotles über die Aristotlishe Theorie des Drama*. Although there is nothing substantially original about

Bernays's therapeutic interpretation of catharsis, since his idea was antici-
pated by Henry Weil (1848), and in effect by Renaissance critics, his
influence on the debate on catharsis has been monumental. A prominent
philologist, Bernays's impact was initially confined to classical scholarship, but his influence on Freud, and the subsequent "cathartic treatment," secured Bernays and his therapeutic interpretation of catharsis an
unchallenged status in the history of aesthetics and psychoanalysis. Bernays argued that catharsis is the purgation of emotions, and he contended
that the pathological effect of tragedy on the "mind would be more naturally elucidated by reference to the effect of medicine on the body."
Bernays also claimed that in drama we associate the homeopathic cure we
feel with the way we "universalize" our emotion. That is, our emotions are
not directed to something related to ourselves, but to experiences we
share with others.[16]

   In 1909, Ingram Bywater also adopted the medical metaphor, and his
translation of the catharsis phrase has become the standard accepted
translation for commentators who adhere to the medical interpretation:

> A tragedy, then, is the imitation of an action that is serious and also, as having
> magnitude, complete in itself; in language with pleasurable accessories, each
> kind brought in separately in the parts of the work; in a dramatic, not in a
> narrative form; with incidents arousing pity and fear, wherewith to accom-
> plish its catharsis of such emotions.[17]

Bywater knows the difficulty in translating catharsis. He asks the question: should or could one understand the term "as a physiological
metaphor, in the sense of 'purging' or 'clearing away'"; or "as a metaphor
from the religious rite of lustration, in the sense of purification?" He ends
by decidedly favoring the physiological metaphor.[18] According to the
critics who believe catharsis to be a medical metaphor, the theater becomes a sort of medicine necessary to produce catharsis to relieve the soul
of pent-up emotions. As relief comes gradually to the spectator, there is
an accompanying harmless pleasure associated with the process of discharge. The spectator at the end of a well-performed, well-written
tragedy feels a kind of relief, a feeling of satisfaction, *stasis*, or harmony as
if relieved of a burden.

   A second significant meaning of catharsis has been moral, or ethical,
a meaning that originated in the Renaissance and subsequently dominated Italian criticism and criticism elsewhere in Europe up to the end of
the eighteenth century. Such meaning was defensive, an attempt to defend literature from attacks against its immorality and irresponsibility.
The need to justify imaginative literature was constantly derogated, and

was treated with distrust even by the very people "in whom the critical faculty might be supposed."[19] In other words, its supporters defended literature by affirming its value as a vehicle for advancing moral ideas. And this is where the explanation of literature as conducive to virtue fits in with the intellectual concerns of the age. Giraldi Cinthio (1504–73) argued:

> Tragedy, whether it has a happy conclusion or an unhappy one, by means of the pitiable and the terrible, purges the minds of the hearers from their vices and influences them to adopt good morals.[20]

Another version of the ethical effects of tragedy is offered by Robertello who believed that the audience, which witnesses atrocities on the stage, becomes accustomed to sorrow and fear, and thus these emotions gradually diminish.[21] Julius Caesar Scaliger (1484–1558), the spokesman for moral values in Renaissance literature, thinks that the aim of all poetry is ethical, in that the poet teaches us to imitate the good and abstain from the bad. Scaliger, however, thinks that catharsis is restricted to few subjects, and not all tragedies produce this effect.[22]

The Renaissance views about the function of tragedy were extended in the seventeenth century by the Neo-Stoics who

> demanded a purgation from tragedy in which the spectator is led by means of fear for himself to resist the approaches of passion in his breast, lest the passion overcome his reasoning faculty and lead him into evil ways. Tragedy demonstrated the dangers resulting from action based upon passion.[23]

The ideas of the Neo-Stoics were opposed in the eighteenth century by the Sentimentalists who emphasized the role of tragedy as a tool to increase compassion. This does not mean, however, that all the Neo-Classical critics of the eighteenth century adhered consistently to one view; on the contrary, some of the major critics of the time oscillated from one view to another.[24] Although Dryden never used the term catharsis itself, he frequently makes reference to "pity and terror":

> [He] commonly interprets Aristotle to mean that tragedy gives rise to pity and terror . . . occasionally takes the medical analogy more literally, and occasionally attempts a compromise . . . ("to expel arrogance, and to introduce compassion").[25]

Dryden's eclectic positions reflect the anxiety and uncertainty of an age that on the one hand skeptically distrusted emotions and, on the other hand, appealed to reason. Paradoxically, however, it was impelled by the mounting force that increasingly emphasized man's emotions. Dryden's ideas clearly point toward the advent of what we often call Romanticism, with its emphasis on "emotions," "feeling," "spontaneity," and "originality," as opposed to "reason," "judgment," "decorum," and "rules."

In the Romantic period, both literature and criticism made the poet the center of imaginative activity. Consequently, for the first time in the history of literary criticism we hear of the "author's catharsis." The poet relieves his tension by writing out his worries, a formula that many Romantic poets and critics subscribed to, such as Byron, Keats, William Hazlitt, Goethe, and John Keble. The most representative statement about the poet's catharsis is Keble's declaration that poetry "gives healing relief to secret mental emotion."

Despite their concern for "transcendental" truths and their constant references to the mind of the poet and how it "transcends" the concrete, material world, the Romantics expressed a cathartic view of art in different ways. In most cases, the Romantics thought that art basically served as a means of personal therapy. Referring to the anxiety that accompanies the composition of a poem, Byron declared that "it comes over me in a kind of rage every now and then . . . and then, if I don't write to empty my mind, I go mad."[26] Shelley with his Platonic idealism affirms in his *Defence of Poetry* (1821) that "tragedy delights by affording a shadow of that pleasure which exists in pain."[27] Although Shelley is ambiguous in this statement as to whether he is referring to the author or the reader, the Romantics mostly thought of catharsis in terms of the author, although occasional reference is made to the catharsis of the audience.[28]

We have dealt so far with some of the critics and commentators who rely on all the information available about catharsis to translate the term into "purgation," "cleansing," or "purification," with medical, moral, or psychological connotations.

II

The second definition of catharsis depends entirely on the use of the term in Aristotle's *Poetics*. This approach is essentially a recent development and corresponds to more recent critical theory.

In August 1936, an article appeared in *Modern Philology* by Richard McKeon entitled "Literary Criticism and the Concept of Imitation in Antiquity."[29] The article caused a major reevaluation of the way critics dealt with Aristotle's *Poetics*, despite the fact that catharsis is never mentioned in the article. McKeon develops an elaborate theory of Plato's system of knowledge and use of terms, and he contrasts his findings with Aristotle's method and terminology. Commenting on the way both Plato and Aristotle use terms, McKeon offers the following acute observation on "imitation," a term with implications closely related to catharsis:

> Whereas for Plato the term "imitation" may undergo an infinite series of gradations of meaning, developed in a series of analogies, for Aristotle the term is restricted definitely to a single literal meaning. In the second place and as a consequence of the first difference, where for Plato an exposition of the word "imitation" involves an excursion through all the reaches of his philosophy, "imitation" for Aristotle is relevant only to one restricted portion of the domain of philosophy and never extends beyond it.[30]

McKeon observes that Aristotle, unlike Plato, consistently defines his terms narrowly, restricting his definitions to the area of knowledge in which he is working. According to McKeon, Aristotle's method is based on the "literal definition of terms" and on the division of knowledge into the theoretical sciences—metaphysics, mathematics, and physics; the practical sciences or the sciences of action—ethics and politics; and the poetic sciences. Each science has its own proper principles, terms, and methodology defined according to the science with which it is associated.[31] McKeon, therefore, would disagree with the critics who rely on the passages in the *Politics* which treat music as a key to understanding what Aristotle says in the *Poetics*. Obviously alluding to the much-disputed catharsis phrase and the way critics have used the phrase as it appears in the *Politics* to explain the meaning of catharsis in the *Poetics*, McKeon gives the following warning:

> To cite what is said concerning art in the *Politics* in refutation or in expansion of what is said on the same subject in the *Poetics*, without recognizing that the one is a political utterance, the other an aesthetic utterance, would be an error comparable to looking for evolution or refutation between the statements of the *Republic* and the *Laws*, without recognizing that the one has reference to a perfect state, the other to a state possible to men as they are.[32]

McKeon's statements about Aristotle's methodology and precise definition of terms led to a new direction in the hermeneutics of "catharsis."

A direct consequence of McKeon's observation was that several critics and commentators began to rely exclusively on the *Poetics* to explain catharsis. Notable among these critics are G. F. Else, Leon Golden, O. B. Hardison, and H. D. F. Kitto. These critics attempted the difficult task of explaining the *Poetics*, its terms and its topics, as an independent, autonomous, self-contained body of knowledge that cannot, or at least should not, be explained by reference to other Greek words, other philosophers, or even by reference to other works by Aristotle himself. Else apparently initiated the move to define Aristotle's *Poetics* without referring to "external evidence" in his influential study, *Aristotle's Poetics: The Argument* (1957). He tries to understand Aristotle's seminal work on its own terms; he, and others like him, do not speculate on a second putative lost book pertaining to the explanation of catharsis, nor do they regard Aristotle's treatise an answer to the charges against poetry put forward by Plato in the *Republic.* In other words, according to the system of thought adopted by Else and his followers, catharsis can be defined only in its context in the *Poetics.* Furthermore, they explain the *Poetics* as a category within the overall Aristotelian system of knowledge, which is based on the division of the domains of knowledge, each with its own appropriate terms and meanings appropriate only to itself. Such a method of understanding Aristotle corresponds to modern Formalistic critical movements, which postulate a work of art as an organic unity. In this way, modern interpretations of Aristotle's catharsis are a reflection of the contemporary critical climate.

After rejecting all the previous interpretations of catharsis because of the inherent problems associated with reliance on external evidence, Else offers the following interpretation:

> Catharsis is not a change or end-product in the spectator's soul, or in the fear and pity (i.e., the dispositions to them) in his soul, but a process carried forward in the emotional material of the play by its structural elements, above all by the recognition. For the recognition is the pay off, to use a vulgar but expressive modernism; or, in a more conventional figure, it is the hinge on which the emotional structure of the play turns.[33]

Else ends by translating "catharsis" as "purification" or "lustration" of certain kinds of actions rather than the purgation or purification of the emotions of the spectator. The emphasis shifts from the audience to the structure of the tragedy. As Else says, catharsis is nothing but an "operational factor within the tragic structure."[34] Else also rejects the notion that catharsis is the end product of tragedy. Characteristically enough, Else translates the catharsis phrase in the following manner:

> Tragedy, then, is a process of imitating an action which has serious implications, is complete, and possesses magnitude; by means of language which has been made sensuously attractive, with each of its varieties found separately in the parts; enacted by the persons themselves and not presented through narrative; through a course of pity and fear completing the purification of tragic acts which have those emotional characteristics.[35]

According to Else's interpretation, the emphasis of the tragedy shifts from the effects of fear and pity on the spectator (or reader) to the understanding of the action; it is a shift from the emotions to the intellect. And it is a shift from a consideration of an aesthetic problem to one that is textual. Although this original approach did not pass unchallenged, it nevertheless opened the way for a deluge of new interpretations, all of which were characterized by their emphasis on the intellect of the spectator or reader rather than on the emotional response.[36]

One of the repercussions of Else's interpretation of Aristotle's *Poetics* was a new translation of the *Poetics* by Leon Golden, who gives a new meaning of catharsis based on Else's conclusions, without offering the same interpretation. Golden gives the following alternative to Else: the poet selects incidents with fear and pity embedded in them; these, then, are presented in a single action governed by the principles of necessity or probability. When the spectator witnesses a tragedy of this kind (which has fear and pity and is governed by the principle of probability) he will learn something from the play; the spectator will enjoy seeing the incidents clarified; and learning, according to Aristotle, is enjoyable.[37] Golden suggests the "clarification" theory to explain Aristotle's catharsis. He also emphasizes intellectual understanding of the actions of a tragedy on the spectator's or reader's part. Golden repeatedly warns against relying on external evidence to support an intellectually-oriented interpretation. He differs somewhat from Else in trying to amalgamate a Formalistic approach with traditional philological investigation to search for the "real" meaning. Although he frequently says that the interpretation of the *Poetics* should come out of the *Poetics* itself and not from any cross-reference, he actually finds support for his views in Aristotle's concern for the intellect not only in the *Poetics*, but elsewhere. He also thinks that his views on catharsis are consistent with Plato's use of the term, and thus represents Aristotle as answering Plato's charges against poetry, or, more accurately, he says Aristotle's ideas are colored by Plato's thinking.[38] Although Golden differs slightly from Else, the essential point is that he relies only on the *Poetics* to interpret catharsis.

H. D. F. Kitto offers another direction for interpretation. Although he bases his argument on Else's theory of intellectual understanding of action, he challenges Else's position by bringing in a related idea that is more traditional than Else's.[39] Kitto argues that catharsis is based on mimesis:

> It is not the emotions of the audience that are purified, purged, or otherwise disposed of; it is the pitiful or frightening *incidents* to which this happens; and what brings it about is the mimesis, the act of representation.[40]

Kitto justifies his interpretation of catharsis through mimesis on these grounds: if suffering does not invoke pity and fear, according to Aristotle, then the action is not tragic; it is the economical use of mimesis that approximates and finally heightens the emotional impact of an incident by eliminating the details that distract and confuse. Within Kitto's concept of mimesis real life actions are not considered tragic because they are accompanied by a lot of details and complexities; it is only through mimesis that those actions are brought into focus by eliminating distracting details that make the action in real life fuzzy, hazy, or confused. Furthermore, mimesis gives the tragic action, as opposed to real life action, "a certain clear direction to our emotion" because "the corresponding event in real life would be . . . noisy and confused."[41] An event in tragedy becomes sharply focused because our attention is directed toward that action alone and not to the other superfluous details that accompany it and create its roughness and untidy edges. It is for this reason that "the action represented in art is more unified, more logical, more significant, more 'serious and philosophic' than an event in real life."[42] Kitto goes on to explain that "mimesis clears away everything but what is meaningful" in an action, and thus it can "enter our mind and bear fruit." Kitto also emphasizes the facts that his interpretation of catharsis and the way he relates it to mimesis are consistent with the *Poetics* as a whole, and that such an interpretation does not rely on external evidence. Although he, also, tries to amalgamate old theories of art with Else's approach, the point is still that catharsis is defined essentially in a Formalistic, intellectual way as clarification. We can also see in Kitto how McKeon's comments on Plato's and Aristotle's definitions of mimesis have found their way to the related subject of catharsis.

We have dealt so far with the three basic interpretations of Aristotle's catharsis: purgation, purification, and clarification. Although there are other modern interpretations that could be considered, some are so far-fetched and esoteric as to render them negligible. For instance, one study interprets catharsis as "the salvation of the hero through faith."[43] Another suggests that catharsis does not refer only to the audience, but also to the purgation of the author and actors of the tragedy.[44] Still another suggests that catharsis refers to the "positive restoration of a beneficial general condition rather than the mere riddance of impurities or harmful elements."[45] One critic has developed an elaborate theory of catharsis based on anthropological criteria.[46] Such a theory views catharsis as a redemptive process, whereby the hero is purified through his suffering and increased understanding of the world and of himself, and the audience shares this insight with him. The tragic hero rises and then falls, and in his fall he is redeemed.[47] The spectator sees the failure and the redemption or salvation of the hero, and recognizes the existence of a divine "wholly other" in the universe. This gives rise to awe or fear and pity, which are intensified when the spectator sees the fall of the hero and his final salvation. Catharsis thus bridges the gap between man and God, and in this sense catharsis restores "some positive relationship between the individual and the supernatural."[48] Most of these interpretations are variations on either traditional approaches, which emphasize an aesthetic view, or the Formalistic approach, which emphasizes a textual or performance approach. The anthropological interpretation is interesting in that it combines Formalistic, aesthetic, and religious approaches. If such a view were to be adopted, the use of catharsis in religious rites would have come full circle from the use of catharsis in connection with ancient Greek ritual. The movement toward transcendence embodied in such an interpretation reflects thought that is religious in its orientation, a contemporary concern.

III

The history of literary theory can be understood, without oversimplification, as a dialectic: the first position is that literature is a tool of some value in defining relationships of individuals with society, morals, education, or the general human condition, whatever that may be. The second position regards literature as artifact. Its sole purpose, its raison d'être, is its enjoyment. The first view expresses what can be called a "functional" view of literature; the latter view in its extremity expresses the basic idea behind the doctrine of "l'art pour art," which emphasizes pure aestheticism. The functional aspect of literature can be better understood in "cathartic" terms: literature has a positive function in our lives, both as individuals and as members of institutions, whether intellectually, morally, educationally, psychologically, or in some other way. That is, literature, in its broadest sense, somehow defines, shapes, or expresses the individual's relationship with others and with his environment. All these concepts, as we have seen in the previous pages, have been labeled "catharsis" by different critics in different times.

Although the term catharsis has been abused, confined, or neglected, the concepts embodied in it have been vital in literature and its interpretation because they convey and express the essential tension between the three angles of the "aesthetic triad": the poet, the poem, and the reader.[49] These three elements come into being through the creation of a poem, and its recreation in the mind of the reader. Creation is a process, the poem is an artifact, and the reader's or spectator's recreation is a process. The two processes (creation and recreation) are by no means identical, nor are they governed by mirror-image rules. Catharsis causes a change in the reader's state of mind (what the Greeks called *stasis* and what in Latin is called *status*). That is, a reader's statis A becomes during and after a reading stasis A + B. The end product of a process that leads to catharsis is that the poem in the reader's mind cannot simply be stasis A, but eventually stasis A + B. B is here the different variables that interfere or work when the poem is read, whether these variables are social, cultural, aesthetic, or psychological.[50] The process of recreating the poem brings into play the different variables just mentioned. For this reason, one single work elicits a Marxist reading, a psychological interpretation, a sociological view, or other different ways of looking at the same text.

This study is primarily concerned with catharsis as an aesthetic response that consists of two elements: 1) emotional arousal and 2) cognition. Different critics and different schools of criticism value either the emotional arousal or the cognitive side of the aesthetic experience, not both. Psychological critics emphasize the emotional side, Formalist critics the cognitive. Both end up being reductionistic as far as catharsis is concerned. The critics who emphasize the emotional side make the aesthetic experience a hedonistic one; those who emphasize the cognitive side impose complete emotional detachment on the part of the audience, thus failing to recognize that cognition in the aesthetic experience is possible only through identification and emotional arousal.

Despite its different interpretations, catharsis has been largely confined to literature, but it is only in psychoanalysis, and particularly in the writings of Sigmund Freud, that catharsis undergoes significant changes. Freud accepts Bernays's interpretation of catharsis as a starting point, only to change it drastically, ending up by making catharsis a cornerstone of modern psychoanalysis.

CHAPTER **2** Catharsis in
Psychoanalysis

> Neither in my youth nor later was I able to detect in
> myself any particular fondness for the position or work of
> a doctor. I was, rather, spurred on by a sort of itch for
> knowledge which concerned human relationships far
> more than the data of natural science.
>
> —FREUD

SINCE THE Renaissance, when Aristotle's *Poetics* was translated into Latin, the concept of catharsis has been the concern of literary critics, aestheticians, philosophers, and scholars involved in classical studies. The concept has oscillated between such interpretations as "purgation," "classification," and "cleansing," among others, but it is only in psychoanalysis that the concept undergoes significant modifications. These modifications not only expand the concept by giving it a psychoanalytic frame of reference, but later color the concept almost exclusively with heavy psychological connotations. No wonder that such disparaging labels as "psychologistic" and "psychologisms" are often used by some critics to belittle Freud's impact on literature in general, and on catharsis in particular. Before we assess such significant changes evolving from Freud's use of the term, we have, therefore, to study the contributions made to catharsis by Sigmund Freud, the founder of psychoanalysis.

[26]

A. The Year 1880, Freud, and the
Beginnings of Psychoanalysis.

We have already discussed Jakob Bernays's contribution to catharsis and his emphasis on the therapeutic function of tragedy. Bernays's interpretation of catharsis can be traced to Milton and even to the Renaissance. His main argument was that it is false to interpret Aristotle's catharsis as purification *through* the emotions; catharsis is the purification *of* the emotions. When Bernays's treatise on catharsis appeared in 1857, it was so popular that eventually a second edition appeared in 1880. By that time the topic had become so widespread and controversial that catharsis at the time "was one of the most discussed subject [sic] among scholars and was the current topic of conversations in Viennese salons."[1] The popularity of the subject of catharsis and the controversy about it was so overwhelming that few people remained interested in discussing the history of drama.[2] It was at this time, in the middle of such discussions and debates, that Dr. Joseph Breuer began his treatment of a highly cultivated Viennese girl suffering from hysteria, known in the history of psychoanalysis as Anna O. Because of their cultural backgrounds, both patient and physician were almost certainly aware of the then current discussions of catharsis. Moreover, Dr. Joseph Breuer in the literature of psychoanalysis is not known to have treated any patient other than Anna O. for hysteria or any other psychological disturbance.[3] It may be true that the popularity of Bernays's treatise on catharsis encouraged both patient and physician to experiment with catharsis as a therapeutic procedure, but Ellenberger asserts that it was Anna O. who dictated her own method of treatment by Dr. Breuer:

> It was one of those cases . . . in which the patient dictated to the physician the therapeutic device he had to use, prophesied the course of the illness, and announced its terminal date.[4]

Breuer called his method of treatment the "cathartic method," and it was essentially a simple one: at the beginning the patient was put under hypnosis, and then she was encouraged to relate the incidents and painful memories that caused her problems. Later on, hypnosis was discarded, and instead the patient was encouraged consciously to recall the painful incidents that caused her symptoms. Ernest Jones argues that "Anna O. was the real discoverer of the cathartic method."[5] Freud met Breuer in that decisive year, 1880. Breuer treated Anna O. between 1880 and 1882; in 1882 he described Anna O.'s case to Freud. The relationship of Freud to catharsis becomes even more involved when we learn that in April 1882, Freud met Martha Bernays, the woman who became his future wife. Jakob Bernays was her uncle.[6]

There is evidence that Freud and Breuer both discussed the method of treating Anna O.; in an article entitled "Hysteria," which Freud wrote for an encyclopedia in 1888, Freud referred to "Breuer's method" in which

> the patient is put under hypnosis back to the psychological pre-history of the ailment and [the physician] compels him to acknowledge the physical occasion on which the disorder in question originated. This method of treatment is new.[7]

Breuer's cathartic method and his findings had not been published by him or anyone else up to this date (1888). It was only when Breuer and Freud jointly published a paper on hysteria (1893), which later became the first chapter of *Studies in Hysteria* (1895), that the cathartic method became well known. What Breuer had done, or rather what Anna O. had told him to do, was to put her under hypnosis. Her morbid symptoms disappeared when their origin was found and when they could be explained. Later Anna O. did not need the hypnosis, because "talking" alone served a function similar to that of hypnosis. She called such treatment the "talking cures," and "chimney-sweeping"; she also used to say that her symptoms were "talked away."[8] After almost two years of "talk cure" Anna O. terminated her treatment. Were it not for Freud, who was fascinated by Breuer's story, and probably by the first practical application of the theoretical interpretation of catharsis, Anna O.'s case might have been buried for ever.

During the time of Anna O.'s treatment (1880–82), Freud worked at the General Hospital in Vienna. In 1885, he decided to study hypnosis under the great master Jean Martin Charcot, who introduced him to "hysteria." Charcot treated hysteria with hypnosis. He tried to impose his will on his patients, ordering them to renounce their symptoms. Breuer, unlike Charcot, allowed Anna O. to express her feelings under hypnosis; he asked Anna O. to "recall and re-enact the traumatic experiences that produced hysteria."[9] Freud told Charcot about Breuer's method, but Charcot showed little interest. After Freud's return in 1886 to Vienna from Paris, he began in 1887 to experiment with hypnosis. In 1889 he used Breuer's method rather than Charcot's. That is, he encouraged the hypnotized patient to recall all the traumatic experiences and memories that led to the symptoms from which the patient was suffering. Anna O.'s case was still vivid in Freud's memory; what fascinated him in the case were the sexual factors, "both in the patient's case history and [in] the development of a marked affection for Breuer."[10]

Breuer contributed one case history to *Studies in Hysteria* (1895); Freud contributed three complete histories and five fragments of cases. Freud's experimentation with catharsis under hypnosis in *Studies* began gradually to diminish, so that by the time he treated Lucie R. (that is, three years after he began the cathartic treatment) he reports that Lucie could not be hypnotized, that he was "obliged to forego somnambulism, and [that] the analysis was made while she was in a state which did not, perhaps, differ much from the normal."[11] Besides Lucie R., Freud appears to have given up hypnosis in two more cases, conducting each treatment in normal conversation. When the patient reached the stage where she was unable or unwilling to remember, he used the "head pressure" technique, which he described as follows:

> I placed my hands on the patient's forehead or took her head between my hands and said: "You will think of it under the pressure of my hand. At the moment at which I relax my pressure you will see something in front of you or something will come into your head. Catch hold of it. It will be what you are looking for. Well, what have you seen or what has occurred to you?"

Later, however, Freud found that he could discard the "head pressure" technique, and that patients were capable of recalling every incident and experience through "free association," in which the patient is encouraged to recall and relate every single incident that occurs to him, no matter how trivial or irrelevant to the particular experience he is trying to remember.

Before studying Freud's impact on "catharsis," we need to investigate the meaning of cathartic treatment, and the method Freud adopted to fit catharsis into his psychology.[12] The theoretical basis of the cathartic treatment as practiced by Breuer and Freud was rather simple: if an experience is accompanied by a large amount of affect (strong emotion), then that experience is overcome only when that affect is discharged (expressed). In hysteria, for reasons unknown at the time, the affect is "strangulated" (barred from expression), thus forcing it to follow a devious route to an outlet, causing the hysterical symptoms. Hypnosis reverses the process: the affect is recalled, and expressed, and thus the symptoms disappear. The process of removing the symptoms is called "abreaction" and the cure "catharsis"; therefore, "the mind clears off (catharts) the unconscious load (often called a complex)."[13] Brill offers the following translation:

The reaction of an injured person to a trauma has really only then a perfect "cathartic effect" if it is expressed in an adequate reaction like revenge. But man finds a substitute for this action in speech through which help the affect can well-nigh be ab-reacted (*abreagirt*).

Although Freud draws a line between "abreaction" as a process and "catharsis" as the state resulting from abreaction, there is agreement that both can be used synonymously and that the distinction between the two is not sharp.[14]

In *Studies*, Freud's therapeutic procedure developed from catharsis under hypnosis to "head pressure" and thence to "free association." Although the latter two techniques were conducted while the patient was awake, Freud still called them "cathartic treatment." Later, however, when he relied only on "free association," he no longer practiced the cathartic treatment proper, which is actually hypnosis. In other words, Freud, in giving up hypnosis, which is associated with catharsis, opted for the term "free association." Jack Spector argues that "cathartic therapy . . . might have suggested to Freud a theory of art as therapeutically expressive behavior, not unlike the psychological purgation of Aristotle."[15]

Juan Dalma says that catharsis is "perhaps the axis of psychoanalytic doctrine."[16] Although Dalma does not substantiate this claim, we find a confirmation of the importance of catharsis to psychoanalysis in Freud's writings. In his preface (July 1908) to the second edition of *Studies*, Freud writes:

The attentive reader will be able to detect in the present book the germs of all that has since been added to the theory of catharsis: for instance, the part played by psychosexual factors and infantilism, the importance of dreams and of unconscious symbolism. And I can give no better advice to any one interested in the development of catharsis into psychoanalysis than to begin with *Studies on Hysteria* and thus follow the path which I myself have trodden.[17]

The study of catharsis is the study of the development of psychoanalysis. Freud himself declares as late as 1924 that "The cathartic method was the immediate precursor of psychoanalysis, and, in spite of every extension of experience and of every modification of theory, is still contained within it as its nucleus."[18]

Freud's "modification of catharsis" is apparent in his "Project for a Scientific Discovery," in which he proposed a "hydraulic model" to explain how stimulations are transformed into psychic energy. The energy resulting from any stimulation leads to filling up (cathecting) the neurons in the nervous system. Once the neurons are filled up, they have to discharge their energy. According to the hydraulic model, emotions build up to a certain extent; if they are not "drained off," they become destructive. Although Freud later discarded this model, in the article he equates pleasure (an aesthetic emotion) with the "sensation of discharge." Freud states his new position on emotions and psychic energy in his *New Introductory Lectures on Psychoanalysis,* where he links emotions to "drives," which he considers the energizing force. There, he seems to imply that expression of emotion provides release of pressure and reduction of frustration.[19]

A similar view is expressed in "The Relations of the Poet to Daydreaming" (1908), where Freud says that a painful experience may lead to pleasure, a position similar to Aristotle's. Freud states that:

> The unreality of . . . [the] poetical world of imagination, however, has very important consequences for literary technique; for many things which if they happened in real life could produce no pleasure can nevertheless give enjoyment in a play—*many emotions which are essentially painful may become a source of enjoyment to the spectators and hearers of the poet's work.*[20]

In chapter 4 of the *Poetics,* Aristotle discusses imitation, and how man "learns his earliest lessons" through imitation, and the universality of the pleasure felt in things imitated. Aristotle argues "Objects which in themselves we view with pain, we delight to contemplate when reproduced with minute fidelity: such as the forms of the most ignoble animals and of dead bodies (Butcher's translation, p. 15). Furthermore, in his *Beyond the Pleasure Principle* (1920), Freud's adherence to the concept of catharsis as the relief that comes from the tension of two conflicting emotions is given a new direction:

> We believe . . . that the course of [mental events] is invariably set in motion by an unpleasurable tension, and that it takes a direction such that its final outcome coincides with a lowering of that tension—that is, with an avoidance of unpleasure or a production of pleasure.[21]

If we extend Freud's argument to catharsis, "pain" and "tension" are conducive to a new state, since the avoidance of pain and tension lead to an aesthetic condition, pleasure. Freud actually had the experience of tragedy in mind when he presented his ideas. He asserts that in tragedy the spectator is not spared the most painful experiences, and yet these same painful experiences become highly enjoyable:

> This is convincing proof that, even under the dominance of the pleasure principle, there are ways and means enough to making what is in itself unpleasurable into a subject to be recollected and worked over in the mind.[22]

Undoubtedly, catharsis is a major concept in the Freudian psychology, but there is a question. Why does Freud later on in his career avoid using the term itself? One of the main reasons is that the early "cathartic method" specifically referred to hypnotic suggestion, and if Freud had given up hypnosis, then it is natural that he would abandon the term associated with the treatment. The problem, however, is not that simple. Although Freud gave up hypnotic suggestion, as early as the *Studies* he refers to the other two methods of psychotherapy—"head pressure" and "free association"—as "cathartic treatments." That Freud did not discard cathartic treatment is stated in a paper entitled "Freud's Psychoanalytic Method" (1904), where he says that the modifications he brought to the cathartic treatment were related to "technique": "The changes which Freud introduced in Breuer's cathartic method of treatment were at first changes in technique."[23] The modifications in technique to which Freud refers are related to head pressure and avoidance of hypnosis, and also to the underlying assumption that in "free association" the patient begins to *understand* rather than merely *relate* his experiences. Free association, which became a standard procedure in psychoanalysis, resembles hypnosis in that the patient closes his eyes, and the analyst asks him to concentrate on certain events, incidents, and experiences, "all of which had at least some resemblance to hypnosis," as Freud himself affirms in the same article (p. 268).

Although the changes in "technique" were the initial step in giving up the cathartic treatment proper ("proper" refers to hypnosis), it is worthwhile to discuss the reasons behind Freud's reluctance to experiment further with catharsis. Freud complained explicitly of at least four obstacles associated with cathartic treatment proper, or, to use an alternative name, hypnotic suggestion. First, not all patients could be hypnotized, so it was necessary to seek a different therapeutic procedure. Second, the therapeutic results were temporary, so that it was necessary to repeat the treatment. Third, the relationship between patient and psychoanalyst should be characterized by trust and faith in the ability of the psychoanalyst.[24] This relationship between patient and psychoanalyst was not an obstacle in itself, since this relationship exists in free association as well; but the relationship was important since it alerted Freud to a phenomenon of great importance in psychoanalysis, which he called "transference." Transference designates the development of an emotional attitude, positive or negative, love or hatred, on the part of the patient toward the analyst. And finally hypnosis does not allow for the understanding of "resistances," which account for the underlying causes of the symptoms. Hypnosis suspends the usual defense mechanisms. R. R.

Greenson has objected to hypnosis because it acts as a form of resistance itself, since it brings the patient temporary relief. Such relief discourages the patient from exploring the causes, the history, and the meaning of his neurotic symptoms.[25] Similarily, Otto Fenichel claims that hypnosis associated with the cathartic treatment has an adverse effect on the patient, because "the patient's ego instead of being enabled to mature is definitively established as immature."[26]

Leaving aside psychoanalytic treatment, Freud's statements on art and imaginative literature were also influenced by catharsis. Freud's posthumously published paper, "Psychopathic Characters on the Stage" (written in 1905), is probably the best short treatment of art and catharsis Freud ever wrote.[27] Its themes are echoed in his other writings on art, and it is important because it relates directly to Freud's statements on catharsis. Freud begins the paper by accepting Jakob Bernays's thesis that catharsis is the "purging of fear and pity," and that this "purging" is the purpose of tragedy.[28] Freud, however, is not content to accept Bernays's formula, and he tries to explain the phenomenon of catharsis through his psychoanalytical findings. Early in the article, he establishes the fact that the phenomenon associated with witnessing tragedy is not restricted to drama but embraces "several other forms of creative writing," such as lyric and epic poetry (p. 306). The experience associated with catharsis comes from the opening up of "sources of pleasure or enjoyment in our emotional life" (p. 305). Such pleasure Freud views as stemming from two sources: one comes through "blowing off steam," which corresponds to the relief felt because of "a thorough discharge," and the second is the result of the accompanying "sexual excitation," which is "a by-product whenever an affect is aroused" (p. 305).

The enjoyment the spectator gets from a play (or any other work of imaginative literature for that matter) comes from his desire to be a hero, and this is why the spectator is led "to *identify himself* with a hero" (p. 305; Freud's emphasis). But the spectator's identification with the hero is qualified: according to Freud, the spectator is led to share the *mental* suffering of the hero, but is spared the *physical* suffering (p. 307). The pain we get from mental suffering is mitigated by the fact that the play is an illusion (p. 306). It is an illusion for two reasons: first, because it is someone else who is suffering and not we; and second, what the spectator sees is only a game out of which he expects no physical harm to his "personal security." Such a notion does not mean that Freud actually trivializes literature, as commonly claimed. "Play," according to Freud, serves a dual function: first, games "abreact" (or cathart) emotions, and then they enable the participant in a game to transcend, as it were, the emotions generated in the play. The participant becomes a master of his emotions rather than succumbing to their dominance.

Freud views the hero as the center of drama. The hero is necessarily a suffering rebel, a rebel against divinity, against social conditions (p. 306).[29] Our enjoyment as spectators, because of our identification with the hero, is "a pleasure due to masochistic satisfaction as well as to direct enjoyment of a character whose greatness is insisted upon in spite of everything" (p. 306). The masochistic satisfaction comes from witnessing "the affliction of a weaker being in the face of divine power," a conflict in which both "the dramatist and the audience take the side of the rebel" (pp. 306, 307). Freud makes the conditions for the spectator's identification with the hero dependent not only on our "willing suspension of disbelief," but also contingent on the might of the "rebel" in us: the more rebellious we are, the more profound is our identification with the hero. If our identification is more profound, then it follows that our catharsis will be more exhaustive, and hence our mastery of our emotions and lives more complete.

Another notion central to Freud's conception of catharsis is of struggle or conflict. Freud links the conflict to suffering. The conflict is not restricted to the dialectic of two opposing external forces, but to the mind of the rebel and to the "struggle between different impulses, and one which must have its end in the extinction, not of the hero, but of one of his impulses; it must end, that is to say, in a renunciation" (p. 308). Freud is not content to define conflict in terms of opposing impulses; he relentlessly pushes the theme further into the realm of the unconscious, making the most enjoyable drama that in which "the source of the suffering in which we take part and from which we are meant to derive pleasure is no longer a conflict between almost equally conscious impulses but between a conscious impulse and a repressed one" (p. 308). If, however, identification with the hero is to be optimal, as Freud insists, certainly the audience should have a least some access to the repressed impulses.

According to Freud, the repressed impulses are universal, in the sense that we all have impulses, and that we constantly repress them. Such repression is not morbid because it "is part and parcel of the foundations of our personal evolution" (p. 309). This is why identification is pushed to the extreme when "we recognize ourselves in the hero: we are susceptible to the same conflict as he is." In a sense, we become the suffering hero; we identify ourselves with the suffering rebel whose repressed impulses the dramatist alludes to, but never states explicitly— impulses that "are never given a definite name." This, according to Freud, explains why the spectator is "carried through with his attention averted, and he is in the grip of his emotions instead of taking stock of what is happening" (p. 309).

Freud's conception of identification can be recapitulated in the following terms: first, the spectator identifies with the hero because we are all rebels; second, our enjoyment is enhanced because what we witness is only an illusion, in the sense that no harm will be done to our physical being, which in its turn mitigates the mental suffering we share with the hero; third, our identification is contingent on the extent of our rebelliousness: the more rebellious we are the more profound our identification will be; fourth, any optimal identification with the hero on the part of the spectator can be traced back to the notion of conflict, more specifically the conflict of repressed impulses. We have these repressed impulses because they are part of our personal evolution.

Freud's contribution to the development of catharsis is unmatched in the history of aesthetics. Although the therapeutic line of interpreting catharsis has always existed, Freud's originality has left indelible marks on the concept in a variety of ways. First, he moved catharsis from the realm of aesthetics to therapeutics: whereas previously catharsis had been almost exclusively restricted to problems related to literary effect, Freud's treatment of the term extended its usage and range of meanings to incorporate the findings of psychoanalysis. Second, catharsis has always been associated with the audience of a tragedy: Freud adapted the term to designate the draining of harmful emotions from the patient in psychotherapy. Third, in psychoanalysis, the term lost its association with the theater and began to point to the psychoanalyst and his consulting sessions, where the patient at the same time became actor and audience. By extending the notion of catharsis to art we see a confirmation of the romantic notion of the artist of whatever kind exorcising his own emotions. Fourth, Freud is the first in the history of literary theory to point out the relationship between catharsis and identification. His insights into identification are developed in the writings of Hans Robert Jauss, the leading theoretician of the Aesthetics of Reception, and will be discussed in chapter 5. Fifth, and probably most important, the aesthetic dimension of cathartic treatment in psychoanalysis and in literature serves two functions: "expression" and "self-mastery."[30] The expressive function of catharsis is associated with what we call "cathartic treatment proper," where self-expression serves its own function. Self-expression is therapy. The function of self-mastery stems from the ability of the patient first to express his emotions, then to realize his problems, then to realize the *cause* of his symptoms, and finally to control his emotions. Freud expressed both functions in discussing children's play in *Beyond the Pleasure Princi-*

ple (1920): "It is clear that in their play children repeat everything that has made a great impression on them in real life, and that in doing so *they abreact the strength of the impression, and . . . make themselves* master of the situation.[31] To "abreact" is the equivalent of to "cathart"; it is the *process* of draining emotions, which is followed by the *state* of becoming "masters of the situation," both emotionally and intellectually (at least in our minds).

For Freud, the making of a work of art is sometimes a safety valve for the artist himself, through which he sublimates his chaotic and elemental drives. Such an action could also be a form of exhibitionism. Freud discusses the notion of sublimating one's suffering into a work of art in his "Goethe Address":

> In what is perhaps his most sublime poetical creation, *Iphigenie,* Goethe shows us a striking instance of expiation, of the freeing of a suffering mind from the burden of guilt, and he makes this catharsis come about through a passionate outburst of feeling under the beneficent influence of loving sympathy.[32]

Freud's notion of art, however, is not simply restricted to aspects as negative as exhibitionism and sublimation. He, in fact, expresses some constructive concepts of art. Rieff says:

> The work of art is, more positively, a means of achieving emotional stability—not weakness but self-mastery. . . . The work of art is not merely a form of acceding to one's feelings; it may also be considered a means of asserting them.[33]

Freud's most important contribution to the development of art is this: when one expresses one's emotions, one gains the power of self-exploration and self-knowledge. The expression of emotion is not detrimental to the intellect, as Plato charges in his *Republic,* but is the eventual path that leads to self-fulfillment and self-understanding. Art is, therefore, to Freud, an important part of our activity, as it serves a function important to our collective and individual psychic health. As such he is on Aristotle's side, but he goes far beyond Aristotle in concentrating on the recipient and the creator of art, rather than on the work itself. It is this foundation that subsequent critics use as a touchstone of belief.

B. The Early Freudians

By early Freudians, I refer to the psychoanalysts who followed Freud's ideas and teachings in the early stages of psychoanalysis, which ended in 1939 with Freud's death. By necessity, such a broad definition excludes the psychologists who "defected" from the psychoanalytic camp, such as Carl G. Jung, Otto Rank, and Alfred Adler. I have restricted my choice of the psychoanalysts in this section to the two who contributed most to the developments, expansions, or modifications of catharsis. Sandor Ferenczi introduced the concept of Neocartharsis, and he will be dealt with in some detail, whereas A. A. Brills's passing remarks on catharsis will receive only cursory treatment.

i. Sandor Ferenczi (1873–1933)

Ferenczi, a Hungarian psychoanalyst, met Freud in 1908, and they were close friends until the former's death in 1933. Ferenczi accompanied Freud and Jung on their trip to the United States in 1910. Although a central figure in the psychoanalytic movement, Ferenczi at the end of his life was almost completely isolated from other psychoanalysts, and within a hair's breadth of a break with Freud. In his article, "Sandor Ferenczi," S. Lorand affirms Ferenczi's independent importance: "More than thirty years after his death, [Ferenczi] is still considered to have made a singular contribution to psychoanalysis, second only to Freud's."[34] According to Ernest Jones, *Studies in Hysteria* remained Ferenczi's favorite reading in psychoanalysis.[35] His interest in *Studies* might explain his innovations in the cathartic method. The long time, sometimes up to four years, needed for treatment caused Ferenczi's dissatisfaction with the method of free association, and so experimented with different methods to shorten the time of treatment.[36] He finally came up with what he called "Neocatharsis" or "active therapy." In the cathartic treatment proper, which Ferenczi called "passive therapy," the therapist asks the patient "to allow himself to be guided uncritically by his ideas."[37] In "Neocatharsis," Ferenczi claims:

> The activity roused in the patient is only means to the end; while the discharge of affect in catharsis was regarded as an end in itself. Where then the task of catharsis ends, the real work of the "active" analyst only begins. (p. 212)

Neocatharsis or "active therapy," in short, applies to adults the methods of child analysis, where the analyst fully participates in the treatment by identifying himself in the closest possible manner with the infantile side of the patient. For instance, Ferenczi says that he assumes a childish manner at the moment when the patient regresses emotionally to an infantile mentality, thus enhancing "transference." With female patients, transference might take the form of sexual attachment, which might explain Breuer's shock at Anna O.'s sexual advances.

Ferenczi's Neocatharsis, as J. A. C. Brown contends, "was entirely in opposition to the Freudian rule that analysts should be as impassive and objective as possible and reveal nothing of themselves to their patients."[38] Late in his life, Ferenczi went to the extreme of encouraging a patient to dramatize his infantile memories, such as baby-talk or playing with dolls, while Ferenczi himself "entered the spirit of the game." Ferenczi realized that the relationship between patient and analyst is reciprocal, and just as there is the patient's transference, there is the analyst's "counter-transference," which can enhance treatment. Extended to art, Neocatharsis can signify the way the audience can "counter-transfer" or influence the author, a notion that has become of particular interest to Marxist critics and to critics of the school of "Aesthetics of Reception" when they study the "production" and "reception" of literary works.

ii. A. A. Brill (1874–1948)

Brill was the first translator to introduce Freud's works and ideas into English. Unlike Ferenczi, he contributed nothing original to the development of catharsis in psychotherapy. As far as catharsis is concerned, his role was that of commentator on and popularizer of Freud's ideas. Explaining literature from the standpoint of psychoanalysis, Brill says:

> Our conception of artistic production as an expression of inner strivings and wishes is not altogether new, for we find it expressed in one form or another in ancient and modern literature alike. Thus, we at once think of Aristotle's famous theory of poetry and drama as a form of catharsis.[39]

Brill, despite his unoriginality, was the first to make, however vaguely, a tenuous distinction between what he called "emotional catharsis" and "mental catharsis," corresponding to Freud's notion of catharsis as "expression" and "self mastery." According to Brill, emotional catharsis is tantamount to venting one's anger and its physical manifestations, for example crying and weeping.[40] A patient achieves mental catharsis through the process of abreaction, when he "abreacts" or works off "the repressed material by living through it and giving free vent in speech and action to the feelings that were originally excluded from consciousness" (p. 62). Although Brill confuses his terminology by calling Freud's and Breuer's abreaction "mental and emotional catharsis," he says that "Aristotle expressed a similar funtion about drama in that it is a mental catharsis" (p. 62).

In short, the following modifications of the term catharsis occurred at the hands of Ferenczi and Brill. Ferenczi introduced "Neocatharsis" to point out the importance of the analyst, on the one hand identifying himself with a situation, and on the other, emphasizing the reciprocal relationship between audience and author.[41] Brill introduced two terms that later psychoanalysts would develop and amplify, the notions of "emotional catharsis" and "mental catharsis."

C. Recent Developments in Psychoanalysis and Catharsis

Since the main purpose of this chapter is to establish the extent to which psychoanalysis early on modified, extended, and developed catharsis in relation to critical theory, I will ignore considerations of catharsis that concern psychotherapy as a field of medicine, and will concentrate only on those "schools" that have a direct relevance to recent critical theory. There are three schools of psychotherapy which are relevant: group psychotherapy, psychodrama, and encounter groups.[42]

i. *Group Psychotherapy*
Group psychotherapy is a term that designates various therapeutic approaches in which one or more therapists treat several patients at once by utilizing group dynamics. In group psychotherapy, "each patient is expected to 'air' his symptoms and his feelings in regard to them. This is termed ventilation or catharsis. He learns to look at his troubles . . . directly and realistically."[43] In group psychotherapy, the therapist and the other members of the group expect the patient to share his intimate feelings, ideas, and experiences with the other patients in an atmosphere of mutual respect and understanding, which, theoretically, is supposed to enhance self-respect and deepen the self-understanding of the group. The origin of group psychotherapy goes back to "mass religious movements and early Greek drama," which, in a sense, moves the concept of catharsis closer to its original association with theater and tragedy.[44] The underlying assumption in group therapy is that a patient will identify with the patients who show emotional arousal most. An important factor in group psychotherapy is "transference," which some psychoanalysts insist on enhancing and encouraging in therapeutic sessions.[45] In fact, S. R. Slavson thinks that transference is a cornerstone of group psychotherapy: "Expression of hostility toward the therapist is a prime requirement in psychotherapy, which should be used in the grist of the therapeutic mill."[46]

The aim of catharsis in group psychotherapy is to increase the patient's emotional awareness, acceptance of others, and expression of emotions and thought. The concept, when extended to art, could designate, I think, the aesthetic value of emotional expressions, emotional awareness, and finally self-understanding: our expression of our emotions could lead us to understand them, and thus to understand our own responses and selves.

ii. Psychodrama

Psychodrama is a method of psychotherapy in which a patient acts out painful experiences and memories. He may perform on an actual stage, taking the leading role, while the therapist becomes the director.[47] This method was developed by J. L. Moreno.

Moreno has acknowledged many times his debt to Aristotle's catharsis as the cornerstone of psychodrama, and Moreno thinks of the Greek tragedy as fulfilling a therapeutic function. The Greeks attended the theater regularly, and thought of tragedy as an integral part of their emotional and cognitive lives, but modern man has lost his ability to communicate with other fellow human beings. Psychodrama, as Moreno contends, aims at providing the modern disturbed man with an opportunity to exercise a sort of an atavistic tendency (reminiscent of the Greeks) by giving full expression to his emotion and anger in hopes of leading to a fuller understanding of them. The technique of psychodrama is thus emotional arousal of the actors or participants that should ideally end in cognition. Early in his career, in the 1920s, Moreno was involved with "The Spontaneity Theater," theater characterized by a shift from written drama to spontaneous (psycho) drama. In such drama the emphasis of catharsis and its therapeutic properties shift from spectator to actor.[48] Moreno offers the following definition for catharsis (taken from his 1923 treatise, "The Spontaneity Theater"): It (the psychodrama) produces a healing effect—not in the spectator (secondary catharsis) but in the producer-actors who produce the drama, and, at the same time, liberate themselves from it" (p. 209).

Moreno uses "spontaneity" in a special sense, and he states that it should not be "erroneously thought of as being more closely allied to emotion and action than to thought" (p. 218).

The various techniques used in psychodrama are characteristically derived from theater: some of the techniques use role reversal, soliloquy, the double, or the mirror. Each technique is used according to the type of patient treated. For instance, an inhibited patient may profit from witnessing auxiliary egos (actors who assist the patient on the stage) performing and imitating some of his own actions on the stage, in which case the technique is called "mirror." Moreno acknowledges the inseparability of

Aristotle's catharsis from psychodrama. In fact, Moreno says that "one of the achievements of psychodrama is the development of the idea of catharsis." Moreno expands catharsis to include the following types: somatic, mental, primary, secondary, individual, and group. Somatic catharsis refers not only to the physical aspect of discharge (such as tears and laughter), but also to what Nichols and Zax call "the rekindling of physical expressivity through action." Mental catharsis refers to the process of re-experiencing and expressing hidden memories of past events. Primary catharsis, according to Moreno, is the catharsis of the actors, whereas secondary refers to the experience felt by the audience when they witness a drama. If catharsis refers to an individual, then it is "individual catharsis," but if it refers to a group of people, then it is "group catharsis." Moreno reverses the ordinary theatrical points of emphasis by calling the actor's catharsis "primary" and the audience's "secondary."

There are two important notions in psychodrama which Moreno is never tired of reiterating: creativity and spontaneity. These two notions, according to Moreno, enable the patient to express, relate, and act out without interruption on a real stage any incident or experience, in order to achieve what Moreno calls "an attempt to breach the dualism between fantasy and reality, and to restore the original unity" to our psyche and emotions.[49] The role of the director in psychodrama is active in warm-up sessions, unlike the detached role played by the psychoanalyst in Freudian "free association." The director provokes and stimulates the actor, encouraging him all the time to take the lead. Once the actor begins the action, the director stays passive, or even "recedes from the scene."

Rieff has argued that "the technique of 'psychodrama' is a reversion from analysis to catharsis. The history of therapeutic debate since Freud describes a full circle back to catharsis."[50] This is hardly so, since what Rieff is talking about is mere emotional discharge, what Moreno might call "somatic catharsis." The objectives of psychodrama, however, are not restricted to expression or discharge of feelings. Psychodrama basically aims at resocializing someone, making him aware of his responses, and enhancing his ability to learn and profit from past experiences. Moreno sums up the practical values of psychodrama in the following manner:

> The ideal objective of psychoanalytic therapy is *total analysis*. It aims to give the patient more analytic insight than the routine of living activates in him spontaneously. The objective of psychodramatic therapy is the opposite; it is *total production* of life, it tries to provide the patient with more reality than the struggle with living permits him to achieve spontaneously, a *"surplus reality."* The excess of life realization helps the patient to gain control and mastery of self and world through practice, not through analysis.[51]

Since more details about psychodrama are beyond the scope of this study, a recapitulation of what has happened to catharsis is worthwhile. Moreno always associates catharsis, a basic concept in psychodrama, with Greek drama and Aristotle's catharsis. Besides the literary and cultural backgrounds on which he bases psychodrama, his method of treatment in which he expands catharsis into somatic, mental, primary, secondary, individual, and group is useful, since it makes catharsis a more precise term; it gives the literary critic shades of meanings that help him distinguish among different associations of catharsis. Literary studies, unfortunately, have completely ignored Moreno's useful distinctions, and the only distinction I know of is the "author catharsis" as opposed to the general reference of catharsis to audience. The vitality of catharsis as a concept, and its concommitant persistence in our critical terminology, makes it necessary to adopt at least variations of Moreno's distinctions whenever reference is made to catharsis.

iii. Encounter Groups

Like psychodrama, encounter groups have their genesis in the humanities; just as Aristotle's catharsis plays the central role in the conceptual framework of psychodrama, encounter group psychotherapy emphasizes catharsis; not only catharsis of feelings but also "cognitive catharsis," that is, understanding, self-exploration, and learning. According to K. D. Benne, encounter groups began as a workshop "on the campus of the State Teachers College in New Britain, Connecticut, during the summer of 1949."[52] The aim of the workshop was to facilitate "the understanding of and compliance with the Fair Employment Practices Act." Most of the participants were teachers and social workers. There were some businessmen and other interested people. A research observer was attached to each group; the observer focused on "coding behavioral interactions." There were evening sessions devoted to the discussion of behavioral events. Soon the "participants reported that they were deriving important understandings of their own behavior and of the behavior of their groups" (p. 83). The phenomenon of "understanding" that occurred was a key to the technique, and thus the small discussion groups, which were called basic skill-training groups (shortened to t-groups), gave rise to a new psychotherapeutic method.

The initial emphasis of t-group was on group dynamics, and the solution of practical problems that faced the participants in their own fields. As a therapeutic method, encounter group psychotherapy emphasizes "techniques of feedback, confrontation, openness, self-disclosure, the challenging of personal values and beliefs . . . and individual dynam-ics."[53] The central theme in treatment is "expressivity, which includes self-disclosure and interpersonal confrontation, as well as emotional expres-sion, ventilation, and discharge" (p. 81). The emphasis is not on venting one's emotions or discharging them, however, but on how to express these emotions in a positive way. Such a notion presupposes two ele-ments: first, the participant should not indulge in mere emotional display, which requires a considerable amount of discipline on the part of the participants; second, the participant should achieve an awareness or understanding of why he had a specific feeling. The aim of encounter groups is intellectual understanding, achievable, sometimes but not al-ways, after some emotional arousal. Nichols and Zax offer the following insight:

> At its best the encounter group methodology integrates emotional expres-sion with an intellectual understanding of the value of expression. Ideally this produces not only an impactful experience, but also insight that can be transferred to life outside the group.

Researchers in such treatment methods give conflicting reports about the effectiveness of encounter groups. J. R. Gibb, for example, concludes that "changes do occur in sensitivity, feeling management, directionality of motivation, attitude toward self, attitudes toward others, and indepen-dence."[54]

Applied to literature, the encounter group method gives us an in-sight into catharsis: catharsis could mean not only the expression of emo-tions or their arousal, but also the understanding of oneself, one's feel-ings, and the value of emotions in one's relationship with others.

The influence of psychoanalysis on catharsis, both as a term and as a literary concept denoting the effect of art on its readers, is massive, both positively and negatively. On the negative side, there is more abuse of catharsis in psychology than use. Cathartic treatment is a simple tech-nique with which any psychologist can experiment. Such simplicity makes catharsis generally associated with the "discharge" of emotions only, and more specifically with physical manifestations such as sorrow, grief, crying, tears, shouting. Two books in psychology that have in their title the word "catharsis" are Nichols and Zax's *Catharsis in Psycho-therapy* (1977), and T. J. Scheffs's *Catharsis in Healing, Ritual, and Drama* (1979).[55] Scheff, rather than developing the insights of Nichols and Zax, offers a simplistic treatment that abuses catharsis. He takes crying, bereavement, and yelling as indicators of catharsis. Rather than concentrating on cognitive-emotional catharsis, he emphasizes what he calls somatic-emotional aspects of catharsis (p. 85).

The second aspect of catharsis in psychoanalysis, which is a positive one, lies in the development, modification, and expansion of the range of meanings associated with catharsis. First, Freud developed catharsis by associating it with identification; catharsis is contingent on the spectator identifying himself with the hero. Second, the arousal of emotions is always accompanied by sexual excitation. Moreover, Freud removes the mere emotional associations of the term and extends it to include intellectual understanding. Ferenczi modified catharsis by introducing the idea of Neocatharsis, which underscores the reciprocal relationships between author and audience. We will see that the School of Aesthetics of Reception in Germany uses Ferenczi's formula and gives it a Marxist turn by expressing it in the following manner: just as production affects reception so reception affects production. Moreno's distinctions of several kinds of catharsis expanded the term and made its different connotations easier to talk about. Rather than relying on the ambiguity of the naked term, we can talk about "cognitive catharsis," "emotive catharsis," "primary catharsis," "secondary catharsis," or "emotional-cognitive catharsis," or any other combinations that help make our references clear, precise, and unambiguous.

CHAPTER 3 Psychological Criticism
and Catharsis

> Psychology shall once more be recognized as the Queen
> of the Sciences, for whose services and equipment the
> other sciences exist. For psychology is once more the
> path to the fundamental problems.
> —NIETZCHE

SIGMUND FREUD's contributions to psychology lead to several modern critical schools of thought, loosely labeled "Psychological Criticism" or "Psychoanalytical Criticism." Freud, primarily concerned with the artist's psychology rather than with his product, thought of the work of art as a means to an end: the artist sublimates his suffering by producing an art work. He thought we can sometimes understand the author's psychology by studying his work, just as Freud himself does in *Delusion and Dream in W. Jensen's Gradiva* (1907). Furthermore, Freud regarded the work of art as a form of exhibitionism. Freud was, however, not exclusively concerned with the artist's psychology. On other occasions, he refers not just to the author but to both text and audience, and the way the audience responds to the text. In fact, Freud equates the literary experience with the notion of play where the participant or audience abreacts (catharts) his or its feelings, thus becoming "the master[s] of the situation." The audience achieves mastery of a situation only if it identifies with the hero, who is, according to Freud, by necessity a rebel.[1]

[45]

Following general practice, I have called the group of critics who derive from Freud's concern with the artist, psychological critics. They take the work of art as the key to the personality of the artist, or the way the artist's personality provides us with insights into the work itself. The second group of critics, those who are mainly concerned with the response of the audience, I refer to as "reader response critics." A classification of critics into two groups such as these is bound to be misleading, since such a categorization imposes or presupposes rigid boundaries of interest and investigation. A single critic, however, may in his writings move from one kind of consideration to another.

My classification merely indicates certain critics' primary concerns. The psychological critics have interests that lie in the use of psychology, of whatever kind and from whatever direction, to account for certain literary phenomena. Such a label does not mean that a critic has been involved in psychological criticism to the exclusion of any other kind. One mark of a good critic is his uneasiness with any single approach. It should be difficult if not impossible to pin down an original work of art by a single approach. Paradoxically, the richest criticism comes from the victory of art over criticism. The more effective the work of art the more subtle and comprehensive the criticism has to be to explain that particular aesthetic effect that the work generates in different readers at different times and in different cultures. If a work yields all its "secrets" to one critical approach, that work, inevitably, is shallow. Kenneth Burke and Lionel Trilling, for example, use different approaches. They are original thinkers who, in expressing interest in psychology, have illuminated usefully the impact of psychology on literature, even through their inclusion as psychological critics does not mean that all or even most of their writings are concerned with psychology.

Psychological criticism has been most successful in that field of literary study traditionally known as "biography." Principles of psychology in general and psychoanalysis in particular have given the biographer an important tool to explain what a work meant to an author at a certain time in his life, and also from such explanation what a work could mean to us. The interest in such criticism is focused on the artist. Ernest Jones gives a good indication of the concern of psychological critics: "Psychoanalysis has actually contributed much more to the psychology of the artist than to that of art itself, but it is impossible to separate the two problems."[2] Generally speaking, literary biographers have emphasized why a certain author chose a particular kind of imagery or theme, and have traced such choices to his psychology.[3]

Some biographers have abused psychology by considering the literary work only as an expression of a neurotic personality; every example of imagery and theme is then reduced and interpreted in terms of neurosis. It is in this particular application of psychology that catharsis is most abused. One example will illustrate my point. In her article, "The Novel as Catharsis," Ruth Morris advances the thesis that "writing," which she equates with what she calls "catharsis," performs a kind of miraculous effect on the morbid personality of the writer. By writing out and thus exorcising his worries, his anxieties, and his problems, a writer is supposed to lead a happy and a balanced life. Typical of such frivolous applications of psychology to literary study is the frequent appearance of the term catharsis, undefined, without any indication of what it means. In Morris's article, incidently, catharsis appears only in the title, and its meaning is left for the reader to define. Catharsis for critics such as Morris apparently means that art is merely an outlet for the draining of excessive energy, a sort of medicinal panacea. Morris cites Kafka as an example of a writer who managed to write out his problems, and thus became mature and balanced through catharsis: "Kafka had lifted himself out of puerility, prolonged boyhood, into maturity through his writing."[4]

The shallowness of such abuses of psychological criticism becomes clearly apparent. In its simplest form, such criticism reduces writing to self-therapy, a long and continuous process that occupies a major part of a writer's life, both in terms of time and energy. Morris, for example, refers on several occasions to the author who "works from an emotional need [and in doing so] heals himself through the process." The notion that writing is self-therapy is self-defeating, however; Morris herself refutes her own argument when she realizes that Hawthorne late in life was "still obsessed with guilt and expiation as if he had not written his earlier works." Clarence Oberndorf refutes Morris's idea on the same grounds, saying: "In most cases, however, the attempt of the author to free himself of the neurosis by writing it out is unsuccessful."[5] Oberndorf, by studying Hawthorne's personality throughout his career, goes on to prove that writing out one's worries does not lead to self-healing. Morris's thesis, that writing is therapy, is not only self-defeating, but also simplistic and reductionistic. It confirms such charges that psychologizing literature is misleading and superficial. But such critics as Ernst Kris, Kenneth Burke, and Lionel Trilling attest to the usefulness of psychology in studying literature and, moreover, prove that psychology when used properly and fruitfully deepens our understanding of how we can employ psychology for a better understanding of literary phenomena and effects.

A study in some detail of Ernst Kris, Simon Lesser, Lionel Trilling, and Kenneth Burke, critics within psychological criticism, shows how each modifies, expands, and develops the idea of catharsis. Of the four, only Kris can be considered a full-fledged psychological critic. Lesser is somewhere between, being a representative figure of psychological criticism and a pioneer of reader-response criticism. The other two, Burke and Trilling, by studying and investigating catharsis, have contributed to our understanding and appreciation of the relationship between literature and psychology.

My choice of these four critics was determined by two factors: first, the depth of the psychological insights each critic has shown in studying literature; second, the unique way in which each critic develops, expands, or modifies catharsis. Such a choice eliminates the consideration of other psychological critics whose contributions to literature have been minimal, or their treatment of catharsis marginal.

A. Lionel Trilling (1905–75)

Trilling, strictly speaking, is a "cultural critic," since his criticism is not concerned with one particular approach but rather with the overall impact of literature on life, and on the way psychoanalysis interacts with or defines culture. His impact on psychological criticism is profound. Louis Fraiberg says of Trilling, "No other critic has shown a comparable grasp of the significance of psychoanalysis; no other critic has so well incorporated it into his criticism."[6]

Trilling believes that Freud is a major figure in defining our culture, and believes his writings, more than those of any critic, challenge and controvert our concept of culture.[7] He has, however, conflicting notions and attitudes about Freud. Despite his deep understanding of Freud and of his impact on literature and culture, Trilling is far from being completely sympathetic with Freud's ideas on literature. In two highly influential essays, "Freud and Literature" and "Art and Neurosis," Trilling quarrels with Freud's ideas on literature.[8] He is particularly critical of Freud's notion of art as "substitute gratification," or as "illusion," or as a "narcotic." He censures Freud for not being able to differentiate between unconscious dreams and artistic creation, and he is most critical of Freud's treatment of the artist as a neurotic. He has gone so far as to say, "Freud's very conception of art is inadequate." Despite his objections, Trilling sees the possibility of literature or art profiting from psychoanalysis in three specific areas: first, Freud's assumption that the mind is a poetry-making organ; second, the concept of catharsis; third, the implications of what Freud calls "the death instinct." The second point is most germane to my purposes since it deals with Trilling's discussion of catharsis, or the way he thinks Freud understood catharsis.

Trilling traces Freud's development of catharsis not to "Psychopathic Characters on Stage" (1905) but to Freud's *Beyond the Pleasure Principle* (1920), where Freud discusses the concept of play and the way it is related to catharsis. He noticed that children do not avoid unpleasant and threatening incidents when they play. Children, in fact, try to recreate these frightening incidents in order to "abreact" their emotions and then to become "master[s] of the situation." Freud finds a parallel to the notion of children's play in adults attending tragedy, in which the audience abreacts its emotions, and its members ultimately gain insights into their lives and emotions through their identification with the hero of a tragedy. In explaining Freud's idea, Trilling takes catharsis to be one area in which psychoanalysis could be most fruitful to literary study, and Trilling affirms that catharsis in Freud "stands beside Aristotle's notion of the catharsis, in part to supplement, in part to modify it."[9] Trilling traces Freud's idea of the function of tragedy to Aristotle, saying that Freud was

> under the influence of the Aristotelian tragic theory which emphasizes a qualified hedonism through suffering. But the pleasure involved in tragedy is perhaps an ambiguous one; and sometimes we must feel that the famous sense of cathartic resolution is perhaps the result of glossing over terror with the beautiful language rather than an evacuation of it. And sometimes the terror even bursts through the language to stand stark and isolated from the play, as does Oedipus's sightless and bleeding face (p. 55).

Rather than giving us Freud's insight into catharsis, or paraphrasing Freud's terminology for us, Trilling, under the guise of explaining Freud, is, in fact, offering a new interpretation of catharsis. First, Trilling rejects the purgation theory, and then once he disposes of the puragational aspect of the aesthetic experience, he is left with the difficult task of accounting for or explaining the existence of the aesthetic feeling we call cathartic (as opposed to the easy task of explaining catharsis as mere evacuation of emotions). Trilling offers a new interpretation of catharsis when he tells us that the particular pleasure we derive from witnessing a tragedy stems from "glossing over terror with beautiful language," and that "sometimes the terror even bursts through the language to stand stark and isolated from the play." These few phrases provide the key to what Trilling means by catharsis.

For Trilling, catharsis does not directly involve emotions or identification. He makes language the essence of tragedy, reducing everything else to a minimum. It is because of the effectiveness of diction that our fear is "glossed over." The audience realizes, comprehends, and interacts with the emotional and intellectual dimension of the most tragic scenes, such as "Oedipus's sightless and bleeding face" because of the beauty of language. Trilling alludes to the description of Oedipus' self-mutilation carried through the messenger's description in *Oedipus Rex.* The messenger's description of the coming horror prepares the audience emotionally and then mentally for the terrifying scene. Language in this context predicts, sets our minds to, and intensifies the visually tragic effect that occurs later in the play. The messenger's description heightens our fear as we anticipate the coming terror. This heightened fear, which builds up as our tension mounts, starts with language. In fact, Trilling implies that the terror conveyed through the messenger's linguistic description is as terrifying as "Oedipus's sightless and bleeding face." In this way, Trilling equates the linguistic effect of the tragedy with its visual one. Indeed, the visual effect alone will be so sudden that it will mitigate the overall mental effect that accompanies tragedy. The final effect, the terror, is optimally achievable by combining both linguistic and visual effects.

If we push Trilling's interpretation of catharsis to its logical consequences, we can explain both emotions and identification in terms of language. The dramatist handles language in a way that insures certain emotional effects in the audience; once the play generates a minimal emotional arousal, the dramatist can enhance this emotional arousal by inviting or arousing the sympathy of the audience. In other words the dramatist has at his disposal a variety of nonlinguistic devices that he employs to make the audience identify with the hero, the action of the play, or the characters on the stage; we cannot say with certainty which aspect of identification Trilling had in mind, nor with whom the audience identifies itself in witnessing a tragedy.

Trilling's linguistically-oriented interpretation of catharsis is weak in one respect. Probably because of its terseness, it fails to distinguish between different levels of identification that different members of the audience experience in witnessing a tragedy, and it obliterates differences in the kinds or levels of aesthetic pleasure experienced by different members of the audience in the cathartic process. Freud's theory of catharsis differentiates between different levels of identification. According to Freud, the more rebellious we are, the more optimal our identification with the hero is. We could argue that Trilling's interpretation of catharsis actually does differentiate between levels of identification if we stretch his conclusions beyond what he actually says. Trilling's differentiation of levels of identification if stretched would be the audience's varying awareness of the nuances of language. The intensity of identification would then depend on each individual's awareness and sensitivity to the metaphors and images that occur in a play, and also to the audience's awareness of the "tradition" of literary discourse. That is, the more an audience is immersed in the tradition of a literary discourse, the more optimal its identification will be. To put it differently, if the members of an audience are acquainted with the conventions of a particular genre, then their acquaintance or familiarity will lead them to a better identification with the hero or incident depicted in that particular genre. When we see a tragedy, we *know* that suffering is corollary to action, we *know* that what we see on stage is not going to lead to self-injury or harm, and we *know* that we are supposed to show a certain decorum in the theater, which has become a social institution.

Such knowledge of tragedy, its conventions, and the theater are not only built into the genre itself, but are also conventionalized or regulated by the particular culture in which a certain genre appears. The Chinese conception and conventions of tragedy, for instance, are indeed different from tragedy as developed in European literature. In both cases, the tragedy as a genre has developed conventions or "rules" peculiar to the culture that has produced it. Trilling's "linguistic" theory of catharsis might be alluding to such conventions, but unfortunately he does not develop his discussion to allow for such a conclusion.

Trilling thinks that his own interpretation of catharsis conforms to Freud's theory of psychoanalysis. He argues that according to

> Freud's theory of the traumatic neurosis [tragedy works within] what might be called the mithridatic function, by which tragedy is used as the homeopathic administration of pain to inure ourselves to the greater pain which life will force upon us (p. 56).

Despite Trilling's appeal to Freud, the function of tragedy which he attributes to Freud is in fact Trilling's own understanding of catharsis and not Freud's. Trilling's mithridatic function takes us back to the Renaissance, specifically to the ideas of Robertello, Minturno, and Castelvetro on tragedy and to the moral interpretation of catharsis.[10] The mithridatic function of tragedy refers to the notion of strengthening the morals of the spectators by allowing them to see violence, agony, and misery on the stage, which will supposedly prepare the spectator to face the fortunes and misfortunes of everyday life.[11] Trilling, unlike a partisan psychologist, does not explain catharsis by relying on psychoanalysis only; he explains

Freud's conception of catharsis by taking the reader back to the mith-ridatic function of literature, an old interpretation of catharsis that en-joyed great popularity in the Renaissance.

B. Ernst Kris (1900–57)

Kris, an art historian who became a professional psychoanalyst, has made important contributions to aesthetics drawing on some of the findings of psychoanalysis. His book, *Psychoanalytic Explorations in Art* (1952) is an indispensable tool for any serious student of art and psychoanalysis.[12] It has been rightly called "the most important book on the psychoanalytic approach to aesthetics since Freud himself."[13] Because of his originality, Kris's considerations of many problems involving aesthetics and psychoanalysis will continue to be valid. Kris's contributions to the development of catharsis are threefold: first, he explains the traditional Aristotelian catharsis within the framework of psychoanalysis; second, he advances his own interpretation of catharsis, based on the findings of ego psychology; and third, he investigates the meaning and complexity of the concept of identification, as it is associated with catharsis.

Kris considers catharsis to be "one of the baffling and most complex questions of traditional aesthetics" (p. 45). Like a good Freudian, he accepts Jakob Bernays's interpretation of catharsis as the purging of emotions, an interpretation that Freud also adopted but modified considerably. Kris, however, faces the dilemma of explaining this purging from the psychoanalytic point of view. An unoriginal explanation of catharsis might run as follows: catharsis is the release of the id impulses, the elemental and nonrational drives that strive to control our lives. The purging of the id impulses is in itself both pleasurable and curative, since purging brings harmony and balance to the human psyche by draining off the surplus psychic energy.[14] Kris, however, is not satisfied with such an explanation, and his own formulations of the way catharsis works are based on his and others' findings in ego psychology. He says:

> We are no longer satisfied with the notion that repressed emotions lose their hold over our mental life when an outlet for them has been found. We believe rather that what Aristotle describes as the purging enables the ego to reestablish the control which is threatened by dammed-up instinctual demands. The search for outlets acts as an aid to assuring or reestablishing this control, and the pleasure is a double one, in both discharge and control. The maintenance of the aesthetic illusion promises the safety to which we were aspiring and guarantees freedom from guilt, since it is not our own fantasy

we follow. It stimulates the rise of feelings which we might otherwise be hesitant to permit ourselves, since they lead to our own reaction which, without this protection, many individuals are unwilling to admit to themselves; with many, we know, this is due to educational pressures, which under certain cultural conditions have generally devalued high intensity of emotional display except in regulated and institutionalized channels: Art offers such socially approved occasions (pp. 45–46).

Some glossing of the psychoanalytic jargon is necessary to help us understand this difficult and important passage.

In 1923, Freud published *The Ego and the Id,* and his terminology substantially changes with this publication. What Freud earlier called "the censor," now becomes the defenses operating in the unconscious part of the ego. Freud introduces the "id," "ego," and "superego," not as biological parts of the brain but as mental constructs or abstractions, which give meaning to psychoanalytic clinical findings. He associates the id with the primary process, which is elemental, chaotic, and governed by the pleasure principle (the id seeks pleasure only). He associates the ego with the secondary process, as it is governed by the reality principle; the ego is rational and calculating, working as an intermediary between a person and the external world. The ego prepares and adjusts the individual to the world and reality by curbing the primitive id impulses, and diluting the dominance of the superego. The superego is the person's moral or ethical code. It is largely unconscious, and as it represents social and family values, it is what we call the "conscience." The ego is constantly under tension between the id and the superego. The ego develops defenses against impulses of both the id and superego, and controls cognition, perception, and volition. In short, the ego has, on the one hand, the cultural and social tasks of adaptation, integration, and synthesis between the individual and his primitive impulses and, on the other hand, the individual and his ethical codes.

Ego psychologists, among whom Kris is an important figure, emphasize the ego functions of the personality in clinical theory and practice. They consider a work of art as a complex interaction of the strivings of the id, the defenses of the ego, and the ego activities. According to Kris, when the emotions (the id impulses) are purged, the ego reestablishes itself by getting rid of dammed-up instincts or drives. Catharsis thus provides a means by which the ego gains control over the id. This control brings pleasure to the individual, both the pleasure associated with the discharge of the destructive id impulses and the pleasure of controlling the id. The pleasure we derive from literature, therefore, is both physiological and mental. Physiological pleasure derives from the *expression* of emotions, and mental pleasure derives from the *mastery* of emotions. The id impulses are detrimental to a person's mental health and people are not normally allowed to express them "due to educational pressures." We are allowed to express our emotions only through, as Kris puts it, "regulated and institutionalized channels." These "channels" are imaginative literature, or art in general, and this is why Kris asserts that "art offers such socially approved occasions." Kris makes the function of art to service the ego, a statement undeniably utilitarian, but it is a psychological utilitarianism that explains art and the catharsis it produces as a socially acceptable, useful, and valuable phenomenon that works as a safety valve for the release of the id impulses of the members of its audience.

Kris also explains the traditional Aristotelian catharsis by relying on the findings of ego psychology and the ego functions:

> The process of catharsis Aristotle has in mind is determined by the complexity of the tragedy as a work of art and hence by the variety of reactions it stimulates in the audience. They all can be described as shifts in psychic levels, as transitions from activity to passivity, and as varying degrees of distance in participation (p. 62).

In his explanation of Aristotle's "catharsis," Kris's "shifts in psychic levels" are related to the distribution of psychic energy, where dammed-up impulses need to be drained off so that the individual can maintain an economic balance of impulses. The "transition from activity to passivity" can be explained in the following manner. In the process of purging emotions, there is a physical activity involved in draining off surplus impulses, as when an individual watches a play. Such active physical operations are accompanied by a physically passive but mentally active intellectual identification of the spectator with the action or characters of the play. The audience's participation in the action of a play depends on the varying aesthetic distances that individual members of the audience achieve in such identification. Such passive intellectualization, shown by the spectator (as opposed to the physical activity of purging the emotions), becomes operative only when physical activity diminishes (that is, when the individual's emotions are discharged). Although Kris seems to contradict himself (p. 59), he really does not do so. He says that when the audience recreates the work of art, "the audience passes from passivity to activity" (p. 59). In this statement Kris makes a fine but an important distinction between catharsis and identification. For Kris catharsis moves from physical activity to mental passivity, but identification moves from passivity to activity. The contradiction between the two statements is only superficial, because identification is an early stage in the cathartic process, and if the psychic operations in both catharsis and identification are the same, then there is no need to talk about a difference between the two.

For Kris, the purging of emotions, associated with the early stages of catharsis, is *intellectually* a passive process, but *physically* an active one. Activity leads to the mastery or control achieved by the ego over the id. The ego's control could be *physically passive* but *mentally active*, because we do not perceive the *physicality* of the process; we do not see immediately any manifest physical activity; there is only calm or repose, which indicates ideation, or the mentally active processes of the ego's control over these emotions. But it is almost impossible to indicate when the physical activity ceases and when the mental activity begins. In any case, both processes result in that calm and serene feeling associated with witnessing the ending of a tragedy. Both "activity and passivity" are pleasurable in themselves, because the discharge of psychic energy is healthy (associated with the feeling of getting rid of a burden) and because of the intellectual pleasure that comes from the mastery of the ego over the id. In short, according to Kris, the work of art neutralizes our psychic energy, a neutralization that is identified with aesthetic pleasure.

So far we have dealt with Kris's explanation of the traditional Aristotelian catharsis; now we turn to Kris's own interpretation of catharsis, an explanation that relies heavily on the findings of ego psychology. Kris proposes the following:

> The understanding of the formal qualities of the verse . . . is . . . such that it imposes upon the audience the task of detaching itself from the immediacy of passions evoked. It imposes, one might say, the necessity for more, or more complete, neutralization of psychic energy.

This is an original interpretation of catharsis, but unfortunately too sketchy to be convincing. The problem with Kris's new interpretation of catharsis lies in his inadequate idea of what someone in the audience does or does not perceive. When a person sees a tragedy, he does not solely try to understand the "formal qualities of verse." Identification makes us involved in the action itself, in the plot as it unravels, and in the hero, or other characters on the stage. The "formal qualities of verse" only cause the spectator to get more involved; they are a *means* to a fuller identification and not the end itself. Kris, relying on Butcher's translation of the *Poetics*, quotes the "formal qualities of verse" as "the several kinds of [linguistic] embellishments." Kris takes the embellishments to be "verse and song."

According to Kris, when emotions are discharged, intellectual understanding begins, and the spectator achieves psychic neutralization. Such neutralization cannot occur, however, if the audience does not identify with the hero, as Kris seems to say by emphasizing the detachment of the audience "from the immediacy of the passions evoked." In other words, Kris makes catharsis contingent on the audience's detachment from the *passions* evoked in the play, but it is difficult to see how identification and then catharsis could occur in that order if we detach ourselves from the passions we see on stage. An audience's detachment from the action of a play or from the passions presented in it would immediately make catharsis a mere mental catharsis, because catharsis begins with emotional arousal on the part of the spectator, then moves to emotional identification, which finally takes us to mental or intellectual catharsis. Any break in this chain results in a different aesthetic experience and not a cathartic one. Despite what Kris says, the audience sympathizes with the hero, and the audience feels the terror of the tragic catastrophe. Identification cannot be optimal if we, the audience, do not feel and share the hero's terror.

Kris's final contribution to the concept of catharsis comes from his modification of the concept and from his investigation of its mechanism as a social phenomenon.[15] He draws a distinction between the artist as artist and the artist as individual. According to Kris, the audience identifies with the artist's ego (p.57, n.82). Unlike Freud, who postulates the hero as a rebel, Kris considers the hero only one kind of a wider phenomenon he calls "the leader" whose main role is to reinforce social control, whether in rituals, religion, or politics (p.57). For Kris, the audience considers the leader as an embodiment of its superego. The audience passes from "passivity to activity" when it identifies with the artist. ("Passivity" is the expression of the id impulses; "activity" is the control of the ego over the id.) In passing from passivity to activity, Kris argues, each member of the audience recreates the work of art according to his own personality. In using the term "recreation," Kris refers to the process whereby each member of the audience "has some emotional semblance to that which the artist experiences" (p.59). Kris's statement amounts to saying that the audience experiences what the artist himself felt when the artwork was being created and made. Such an idea is picked up by Norman Holland in his *Dynamics of Literary Response*, as will be discussed under "reader-response critics" in chapter 5.

According to Kris, the cathartic process is associated with a certain aesthetic feeling, which he explains in the following typical passage:

> The ego relaxes control; i.e., it opens the way to an interplay with the id. This phase is predominately passive: the art work dominates the public. In a

later phase, the ego asserts its position in recreation. In doing so, it not only wards off fear of the demands of the id and the superego, but it controls the flow of mental energy (p.62).

What is important in Kris's formulation is his assertion that our processes of response, identification, and recreation of the work of art are all controlled by the ego. There are at least two consequences for such a conclusion: first, the audience's catharsis is not a naive, hedonistic display of emotion (because the audience achieves catharsis only through the control of the ego); and second, the intellectual pleasure that is derived from catharsis stems from the reader's or audience's recreation of the work of art. In this sense, catharsis unites both author and audience through the sharing of similar experiences and feelings. The audience experiences what the author himself felt when he wrote his work.

Kris's other insights into the psychology of art are too numerous and detailed to be dealt with here. His ideas have influenced virtually every critic who has made use of psychoanalysis for the understanding of literature, and we hear his ideas echoed, translated, and even restated by different literary critics. His analysis of catharsis is important because he links catharsis with identification, and because he associates catharsis with the social functions of art. Most important of all is, perhaps, his explanation of the mechanisms of the aesthetic feeling associated with catharsis, an explanation that is based on ego psychology and not on traditional psychoanalysis.

C. Kenneth Burke (b.1897)

Of all twentieth-century critics Burke has shown the most unwavering interest in catharsis. Throughout his career as a critic, he has systematically and insistently addressed himself to the full ramifications and complexities of the concept. Almost every piece of his critical writings in one way or another modifies, expands, investigates, or contemplates the meanings of catharsis.[16] Because of the limitations of space, my analysis will basically rely on two major articles Burke specifically devotes to the study of catharsis.[17] Although such a cursory treatment will tend to oversimplify the intricacies of some of Burke's critical formulations, critical studies of such formulations can be pursued further in at least four book-length studies of Burke's criticism (besides another book on the responses of critics to his criticism).[18]

According to Burke, catharsis is not simply a literary term but, rather, a concept that involves the reader, the critic, society, and man's overall concern with symbols. In this sense, catharsis would be misunder-

stood if studied exclusively from a linguistic point of view. Burke, therefore, investigates the implications of catharsis by studying the three nonlinguistic sources on which the term is based. These sources are

> the human body, the "world's body" (the natural scene), and the body politic.
> (The last would include the whole range of personal and social relations, as
> between parents and offspring, ruler and subjects, doctor and patient, stu-
> dent and teacher . . .) (OCOR, p.338).

Since Burke's conception of catharsis embraces such a wide field, several
ideas and concepts are essential corollaries to Burke's understanding and
treatment of catharsis. The first idea is that of the "pollution" that should
be "cleansed." The second is the inseparability of catharsis from the notions of victimization, scapegoats, sacrifice, and ritual. All these ideas are
given a psychoanalytic turn by Burke's assertion that any "purgation,"
"expulsion," or "secretion" involves some sexual pleasure, a statement
that takes us back to Freud's formulation on the sexual pleasure derived
from the excitation of any emotion. Burke's study of catharsis leads him to
associate catharsis with certain historical and cultural factors. A work of
art that causes a certain audience to identify with the hero does not
necessarily entail the same effects and consequences for an audience with
a different culture, with a different set of values, or living in a specific
historical moment. In other words, Burke makes catharsis, as a phenomenon, moment bound. Although catharsis occurs in manifold settings and
times, it is not a universal phenomenon but a local one; it applies only to
works that specifically address themselves to certain social situations or
social values prevalent in and restricted to a given social group. Burke
confirms such an observation by discussing the effect of the same play on
two politically different audiences. Jean Anouilh's *Antigone* (1944), which
contains allusive references to the German army's occupation of France at
the time of its production, had a carthartic effect when first presented.
When the same play now appears in the United States, Burke says that
"the play would seem to have no cathartic effect whatsoever" (OCOR, p.
362).

Burke's insistence on ritual and victimage might mistakenly lead the
reader to associate Burke with the notion of catharsis as a collective
attitude shown by an audience. Burke himself rejects simplistic explana-
tions of catharsis that emphasize the dynamics of rituals by emphasizing
individual response:

> The centrality of the nervous system is a *principium individuationis*
> whereby, no matter how collective the nature of our symbol-systems and of
> the sociopolitical structures that go with them, our pleasures and pains are
> our own naturally inalienable private property. (CSV, p. 107).

For Burke, no matter how much we share a particular feeling with the other members of the group to which we belong, catharsis is individual. A feeling may be shared by members of a group, but its apprehension is essentially personal.

For Burke, catharsis assumes many guises and shapes with different emotions. One of his original formulations is to explain catharsis not through pity and fear but through love: "Perfect catharsis would arise from a sense of universal love. Insofar as such a condition is not attained, the next best thing is a sense of radical pity that lies on the slope of tearful release" (CSV, p. 109). Burke tries to explain love through pity by relying on Aristotle, but the obvious objection to such a statement is that "love is fullest only when immediately personal," whereas Burke's treatment would dilate the emotion. Although Burke's concern with love as a substitute for pity seems irrelevant to his discussion of catharsis, it is in fact the open window through which he allows Freud to enter his system: "The simplest distortion of love, from the standpoint of catharsis, is the kind of art that would arouse sexual desire sheerly by the flaunting of sexual wares" (CSV, p. 112). Once he has given love sexual implications, whether erotic or agapeic, Burke is capable of linking love to tension, a sexual tension that tragedy resolves via catharsis. In other words, Burke adheres to Freud's concept of catharsis as exciting the emotions of the audience. Freud maintained that any excitation has a sexual pleasure; Burke too emphasizes both the sexual pleasure and the tension that accompanies this sexual excitation. Catharsis is the relief that comes from easing this erotic tension.

Another area that interests Burke is the relationship between catharsis and religion. Because Aristotle's "pity" is translated as "mercy" in the New Testament, Burke asks the following rhetorical question: "Thus, insofar as being pitiful is being merciful, might one not, in feeling pity, feel lordly?" (OCOR, p. 344). Characteristically enough, Burke explains religion through his notion of man as a "symbol-making" animal. Here is a typical passage:

> Since the idea of an infant implies the idea of a mother, pictures of Madonna and Child can be developed to the point where the stress shifts from Jesus to Mary. This development is *internal* to the moment . . . [but] it can introduce an emphasis that some of the faithful will feel as a shift from "Christianity" towards "Mariolatry" (CSV, p. 117; Burke's emphasis).

Here, he points out how symbols change with the change of the medium through which the symbols are conveyed. The mind of the faithful will move from a picture depicting Madonna and Child to Mary as a mother. But in moving from theology to symbols, Burke realizes that "Christianity is not intrinsically cathartic," although he thinks it could be "manipulated" to cathartic ends.

Burke tries to link religion to ritual and to the symbols used in rituals, which, at least, become part of a ritualistic celebration (for instance, the role of the altar pieces in the Catholic mass). He attempts to explain religious rites in the light of Greek rituals, which, for him at least, perform the same purgative effect as the ancient conception of catharsis did (catharsis was associated with Greek rituals). But Burke seems confused when he restricts catharsis to the mere expression of emotion, when he endows religion with "regulatory effects": "In the case of religion, the situation is further complicated by the fact that religion aims to be not solely cathartic, but also regulatory" (OCOR, p. 365).

By emphasizing the regulatory effect of religion, Burke seemingly alludes to a chaotic element in catharsis. Within his priorities, religion is superior to catharsis. But he reverses his priorities elsewhere when he states his aesthetic doctrine by emphasizing three components of art: art is not merely *self-expression communicated* through a medium, but it is the transcendence of self-expression that makes art viable. If we discuss Burke's statement on religion as being not merely "cathartic but also regulatory," we find that Burke violates his own aesthetic doctrine by emphasizing the first two aspects of catharsis only, that it is self-expression and communication. Burke fails to see that catharsis becomes regulatory when it transcends the specific moment that raises the emotions and purges them. Otherwise, catharsis can never be more than the author's self-expression (release, purgation, cleansing, and so on) communicated to the audience.

Just as catharsis is important to Burke's critical system, so is identification, which is in fact an essential corollary to the cathartic process. Although Burke does not discuss identification *per se* either as an individual topic or as an element for the fulfillment of the cathartic process, he makes frequent references to identification, involvement, engagement, and communion:

> Tragic catharsis through fear and pity operates as a *substitute* for catharsis through love. One's state of identification or communion with the object of one's pity is nearly like the kind of identification or communion one feels for a loved object (CSV, pp. 108–109; Burke's emphasis).

Burke, in emphasizing *love* as a substitute for *pity*, makes an original contribution to our understanding of identification. We do not pity the tragic hero, but rather love him through our identification with him. But this is only one of the many ways in which Burke investigates identification.

Another way in which Burke treats identification is by using the notion of "vicariousness," which he employs as leading to the idea of "victimage" (CSV, p. ll8, and OCOR, p. 340). The purgative element in drama, Burke argues, requires some sort of substitution, vicarage, or vicarious victimage, since all these notions are built in the very nature of drama. This goes back to the way the Greeks associated drama with sacrifice and the appeasement of the gods or fate. If we see drama as archetypal, as associated with "sacrifice" and "the kill," our fondness for drama reflects our atavistic attraction to victimage (CSV, p. 118).

A third way in which Burke expresses the notion of identification is by using "engagement," which he links to the Aristotelian concept of *hamartia,* or tragic flaw:

> Since misfortune moves us most to pity when it is undeserved, and since we are most moved to fear when the sufferer is in some notable way like ourselves, the tragic *hamartia* is a remarkably efficient way of engaging an audience (OCOR, p. 340).

By emphasizing *hamartia* as an effective element at the disposal of the dramatist, Burke is making *hamartia* an effective rhetorical way of reinforcing identification. *Hamartia* is one of the traditional ways of understanding catharsis, because it is associated with mimesis; Burke argues along the same line of thought, but reverses the traditional priorities. What makes the protagonist of a tragedy credible or real is his closeness to us, or the way in which we share with him some of our worries and characteristics. According to Burke, the tragic flaw becomes a short cut to our sympathetic identification with the hero.

After discussing identification and the different elements that enhance or reinforce catharsis, Burke turns to the knotty problem of the pleasure the audience derives from witnessing a tragedy. According to Burke, the joy comes from our tendency to like victimage. Such a notion allows Burke to conclude that "closely related to this cult of victimage implicit in the very nature of drama there is the act of vicarage, of *substitution*" (CSV, p. 118; Burke's emphasis). Despite his emphasis on victimage, ritual, and redemption as different aspects of catharsis, Burke interprets all these concepts as occurring within the framework of man's consciousness as a "symbol-making" animal. A point of departure for such a view is the importance that Burke attaches to two words: "cleansing" and "unclean." Here is a typical example:

> People are "cleansed" in one respect when after indecision they hit upon a course of action. They are cleansed in another respect when they become so intensely "inside" to a symbol-system that a new quality of order of motives emerges from within it. And they are cleansed in still another respect when,

the goal having been reached, fulfillment is complete. Each has its own kind of gratification, corresponding to the beginning, middle, and end of a project. They are purely formal aspects of catharsis that do not directly involve victimage (CSV, p. 127).

Burke modifies the concept of catharsis radically here, and we need to dwell on some of the basic ideas he discusses. First, catharsis is not mere contemplation or self-expression, but is the result of a course of action people take after indecision. If they do not, they are not cleansed. Second, Burke equates catharsis with adjustment to culture, a culture that is exclusively governed by symbol-laden values. Catharsis becomes, in this sense, the acceptance of a society or culture reduced or elevated (depending on where we stand) to symbol-processing. Another extension of catharsis occurs when Burke views progression that fulfills an end as essentially cathartic. Such an extension is apparently based on the analogy of action in the broad sense of the word, with drama that has a beginning, a middle, and an end. In both cases—in drama and in action—the result is "gratification," not a haphazard gratification, but a serene one that corresponds to three stages of development, "beginning, middle, and end."
     Elsewhere, Burke discusses his aesthetic concerns by placing himself in the category of critics who are not merely interested in "self-expression" or "communication" but also in "transcendence":

(1) Art begins in *self-expression*, a spontaneous utterance, as with outcries, oaths, interjections.

(2) Such motives are matured by translation into the great complexities of language that owe their development to the use of language as a medium of communication.

(3) But the work of art moves *towards the transcendencing of both self-expression and communication.*[19]

Burke's main areas of interest in catharsis are three: catharsis could be related to the poet, or to the audience, or to the critic (COR, p.366). Catharsis has a therapeutic effect, a social function, and an aesthetic function. All these aspects of catharsis are combined in some key concepts that are inseparable from catharsis, such as "uncleanliness," "purgation," "victimage," "mortification," "transcendence," and "communication," among others. Catharsis is action, acclimatization, and symbol-laden. The extent to which catharsis permeates Burke's critical activity is beyond the scope of this study, but we can say that Burke has contributed to the development of catharsis, changing it from merely a concept or a phenomenon that is associated with tragedy to a phenomenon that embraces literature, the society, and culture, by making catharsis primarily a "symbol-governed" aspect of a literary work.

D. Simon O. Lesser

Lesser's *Fiction and the Unconscious* (1957) is the first book-length attempt by a nonprofessional psychoanalyst to assimilate Freud's writings to literature by applying psychoanalytic insights to fiction.[20] *Fiction and the Unconscious* has been regarded as "a minor classic in psychoanalytic literary criticism."[21] Lesser's understanding and treatment of catharsis is basically Freudian, supported by Ernst Kris's investigations into ego psychology, but his achievement in *Fiction and the Unconscious* is not just restricted to popularizing Freud's ideas: he expanded some of Freud's ideas on literature and modified others.

An important part of Lesser's treatment of catharsis is his emphasis on a reversal of roles. The members of the audience are originally considered as participants and then experience catharsis by shifting their role from participants to spectators: "The experience Aristotle described as catharsis . . . evidently arises from an unnoticed shift of roles—a shift from a stage in which we are predominantly participants to one in which, predominantly or entirely, we are spectators" (p. 248).

Lesser's emphasis on the shift of roles allows him to discuss identification as a sequential process and in terms of several characters on the stage, for Lesser, unlike Freud, does not limit the audience's identification to the hero alone. The audience identifies "in most cases with other characters as well." Neither Freud nor Kris discusses explicitly the time sequence in which the audience's identification occurs, nor when it becomes most intense, nor when it is given up (the audience detaches itself from identification). Lesser, however, argues that identification ceases at the end of the play, and he makes the cathartic relief impingent on that particular moment: "Normally, however, it [detachment] occurs very late, and it *must* occur late if we are to experience cathartic relief. The extraction of the emotional gratification a particular identification permits is the first constituent of the cathartic experience" (p. 249, Lesser's emphasis).

Lesser's idea of late detachment leads to a problem. According to Lesser, catharsis has two constituents: the first is the emotional gratification that accompanies identification; and second, is the "perception of the consequences of the hero's conduct." Lesser argues that the moment the hero is close to his inevitable end, we abandon our identification, and detach ourselves completely from the hero's tragic end "instead of vicariously experiencing it" (p. 249). The problem arises at this point. If the audience were to detach itself from the action, and to abandon its identification before the tragic fall of the hero, then the cathartic experience would not occur. It would thus be hanging in the air. In fact, we could not separate the audience's emotional arousal from its intellectual understanding, because the latter would be a logical consequence of the former, as far as our understanding of the cathartic mechanisms are concerned. If there is too much emphasis on intellectual understanding—which accompanies the disengagement of the audience from the action of the play, as Lesser argues for—then we are dealing with a different aesthetic element, a purely cognitive experience, not a cathartic one. My understanding of catharsis leads me to censure Lesser for his emphasis on intellectual understanding, because if the cathartic experience begins with emotional arousal and if then there is a conflict of two contradictory emotions, and if then the antithesis of such contradictory emotions is catharsis, then Lesser's emphasis on the last stage only makes catharsis intellectual understanding. Intellectual understanding is quite different from cathartic experience.

Lesser's argument emphasizes the detachment of the audience from the tragic incident when the hero is about to fall, because such a detachment will give us assurance and protect us from the consequences of too much identification. What Lesser forgets is Freud's assertion that what we see on the stage is only an *illusion;* it is an illusion because we do not expect any physical harm to our well-being from too much identification. Indeed if it were not an illusion, identification would not exist, and probably no aesthetic experience at all would accompany the tragedy, since we would be endangering our own safety.

Almost two centuries ago, Samuel Johnson faced the same dilemma that worries Lesser. Eighteenth-century critics, particularly influenced by French "rules criticism," insisted on the three unities: time, place, and action. The critics insisted on these unities because they thought they increased verisimilitude. The more verisimilitude, the more the audience would identify with the characters on stage. Johnson exploded the theory behind the rule of the unities by reminding his readers that "the stage is only a stage." In his *Preface to Shakespeare* (1765), he had already solved Lesser's fear of the consequences of identification by invoking what we call aesthetic distance, by saying that we suspend our belief when we read literature, or attend theater: "The truth is, that the spectators are always in their senses, from the first act to the last, that the stage is only a stage, and that the players are only players."[22] Fifty years after Johnson, Samuel T. Coleridge coined the phrase, the "suspension of disbelief." It has been accepted that identification, normally, will not lead us to believe in the reality of the action in front of us; otherwise, every sane person would take to his heels to seek refuge from the dramatic catastrophe he would be witnessing. Only a mentally disturbed person would confuse his aesthetic identification with the sense of reality.

There is, however, a positive side in Lesser's discussion of identification. Identification for him cannot be consistently intense throughout the play: "As our analysis of the cathartic experience suggested, as one reads there are probably many shifts, gradual or even abrupt, in the extent to which one is involved" (p. 266). Lesser asserts that the intensity of our identification with the hero or our involvement in the action of the play is subject to either progression or regression, or as he says to "shifts." Identification can become more intense, or it can dwindle. Although Lesser does not explain why fluctuations occur, we can easily account for the phenomenon by appealing to psychoanalysis. If the id impulses are given free reign in the actual process of aesthetic involvement (reading or witnessing a tragedy) the intensity of identification corresponds to the amount of psychic energy that flows from the id. When the amount of psychic energy increases because of tension, identification becomes more intense; the opposite is also true. In both cases, however, identification never ceases. If it does, to phrase the argument according to Lesser's terminology, no cathartic experience will take place, and if the outcome of identification is anxiety, then anxiety too will not exist. It is the identification of the audience with the characters on the stage that causes our anxieties and conflicts; without it, there is no room for anxiety, a point about which Lesser does not seem to be fully aware.

Lesser's main thesis in *Fiction and the Unconscious* is that fiction appeals to our fantasies and through catharsis appeases our fears and anxieties: "Since fiction strives to resolve the tensions it arouses, reading fiction ordinarily leaves us feeling refreshed and restored, in a good frame of mind for coping with any task which lies before us" (p. 55).

One of Lesser's understandings of catharsis is stated in his article "Tragedy, Comedy, and the Esthetic Experience."[23] He equates what he calls "the esthetic experience" with "beauty," and he is highly influenced by I. A. Richards's ideas in his treatment of the subject, as he himself acknowledges (p. 289, n. 9). Lesser defines the aesthetic experience, which is his term for catharsis, in the following manner:

> The esthetic experience can be nothing else but this—a feeling that all our claims, however contradictory, have been brought into balance and satisfied, a feeling of equilibrium based upon fullfilment rather than the denial of these

needs which cannot be fitted into the more impoverished pattern of living
we have developed for ourself [sic], a feeling of wanting nothing, of having
everything for which we could possibly ask (p. 287).

Lesser affirms that such an experience makes us "feel exhilarated and
refreshed." Furthermore, he does not restrict such an experience to
tragedy alone, but includes novels, short stories, motion pictures, and
musical comedies (p. 290).

A major modification of catharsis occurs when Lesser shifts the emphasis from the tension of emotions (for example, fear and pity) to the
tension between form and content (another insight Norman Holland later
picked up):

> The tension between content and form suggests that fiction tries to satisfy
> divergent and even discordant needs; and close analysis of content and form
> shows that each of them appeals individually to the several parts of the
> psyche (p.290).

Although Lesser elsewhere argues that there is no such thing as
"form" or "content" and argues for their inseparability, he devotes a whole
chapter to the "Functions of Form" (p. 71, 121–44). He assigns three functions to form: "to give pleasure, to avoid or relieve guilt and anxiety, and
to facilitate perception" (p. 125). In short, form communicates content by
maximizing our pleasure and minimizing our guilt and anxiety. Lesser
modifies the idea of catharsis from the tension of emotions to the tension
of form and content, although he does not develop this idea explicitly.

Catharsis, to Lesser, is the outcome of the conflict of form with
content, but before we can reconstruct Lesser's theory of catharsis as the
tension of form and content, we need to understand Lesser's conception
of each, and of the aesthetic values he attaches to them. Lesser, on the
one hand, attaches more importance to content, saying that it gives more
pleasure than the pleasure that comes from form. On the other hand, he
alludes to the idea of catharsis as coming from the interaction of both form
and content: "A driving purpose of form is to transform that which inspires
terror into something which can be contemplated and experienced without fear" (p. 128). Form is thus the means by which a spectator, reader, or
whoever, achieves aesthetic distance and a feeling of security. An integral
part of the cathartic process is the security that the audience feels when it
identifies with the hero of a tragedy. According to Lesser, the terror (or
any frightening emotion) that we witness and feel on stage is transformed
into a quiet mental process (or ideation) of contemplation that the audience enjoys without fear. Surprisingly enough, Lesser assigns such enjoy-

ment to form rather than content, since he has already argued for the importance of content. One way of explaining this impasse is to postulate the following: terror, as it is expressed in the contents of a play, is not in itself a source of catharsis. It is only when the members of the audience feel another emotion that contradicts terror that catharsis will occur. The idea of conflict is latent in such an explanation. Fear, as expressing the content of a work of art, is ineffective unless it coincides with our situation as spectators or readers; that is, when we feel safe and secure. Form directs such fear to our hidden impulses and desires, and the conflict between what we actually see on stage (content) and what we actually feel (form) as spectators leads to the cathartic experience.

Such an explanation of catharsis is an important psychologically oriented interpretation of how catharsis occurs. Unfortunately, Lesser does not develop his ideas far enough to allow us to arrive at a workable definition of catharsis, or how to account for the mechanisms of catharsis within the framework of psychoanalysis. Lesser vaguely explains catharsis in fiction as coming from the conflict of form and content, a conflict which is resolved in catharsis or resolution.

We have noticed that the use of psychology in the explanation of catharsis has two main trends: first, catharsis is linked to id, ego, and superego (Kris, Lesser); second, catharsis is explained through a system based on the notion of man being surrounded by symbols. In the second trend catharsis becomes a focal point in Kenneth Burke's investigation of critical theory and works of art. His understanding of catharsis is insepa-rable from his understanding of such concepts as "victimage," "sacrifice," "transcendence," among others. Another important aspect that comes from applying psychological insights to the study of catharsis is the inter-pretation of catharsis as a linguistically oriented phenomenon (Kris, Tril-ling). Unfortunately, such an interpretation is only fragmentary and sketchy. Despite weaknesses, all these critics attest to the vitality of psy-chological readings of literature. The influence of their discussions on later critics is testimony to the continuity and permanence of catharsis in our critical concerns.

CHAPTER 4 Catharsis in
Formalist Criticism

I would remind [the reader] that I write in an age when,
in the majority of social circles, to be seriously interested
in art is to be thought an oddity.

—I. A. RICHARDS

FREUD'S IMPACT on many disciplines and schools of thought has
been more far-reaching and pervasive than the impact of any individual
thinker in the modern era. In literary criticism, Freud's influence has
been marked by a continuous assimilation of his ideas. But the many
abuses of Freud's insights led to the development of the New Criticism,
an opposing twentieth-century movement that rejects psychological criticism and offers an alternative method of reading and evaluating literature.
Because emotions play a decisive role in psychological criticism, New
Criticism tries to ignore their relevance to the literary work, or at least to
minimize their importance.

The New Critics insisted that literature should be valued without
reference to the reader, to society, or to time. Emotions are not related to
our understanding of the work of art, nor are sociological elements, nor
psychological considerations of author or reader. Since emotions, society,
and psychology are not valid as criteria for evaluating art, the New Critics

argue for the relevance of cognition or understanding. They contend that literature gives us an aesthetic experience that is totally intellectual. Such contentions are deficient from the viewpoint of catharsis. A literary experience cannot begin and end with intellectual understanding. Catharsis presupposes the arousal of emotions, then their reconciliation, and then intellectual understanding.

New Criticism was a movement that, as a defense of literature, opposed psychological criticism. When we see it this way, we can understand why it tried to avoid any mention of emotions and why its proponents abhorred catharsis. We can also understand why two articles pertaining to the basic premises of New Criticism became a sort of literary manifesto. These two articles are Wimsatt's and Beardsley's "The Intentional Fallacy" (1946) and "The Affective Fallacy" (1949).[1] The first article warns the reader not to confuse the literary work with its *origins*, as the Romantics did by thinking of the poem as an expression of the author's self. The second, on the affective fallacy, tells the reader not to confuse the literary work with its *effects*. Both articles assume that a literary work is an autonomous object, its meaning and value unrelated to author, reader, or society. Both articles are also a direct attack on catharsis. The one on the intentional fallacy is an attack on the Romantic notion of author-catharsis; the one on the affective fallacy is an attack on reader-catharsis. But even in their literary manifestoes that oppose catharsis, the term creeps in, and, finally Wimsatt and Beardsley admit that "Aristotle's catharsis is a true theory of poetry, that is, part of a definition of poetry."[2]

Given the connotations of emotive diction, it was difficult for the Formalists to conceive of poetry as not arousing emotions. The fact that the Formalists acknowledged the validity of catharsis in the very manifesto that was intended to oppose catharsis is an explicit acknowledgment of the part of the Formalists that emotions are relevant to our understanding of poetry. Moreover, according to the Formalists, we cannot define poetry without considering its effects. The New Critics tried unsuccessfully to ignore the role of emotions in evaluating poetry, and they implicitly acknowledged emotions as antecedents to cognition. The ways in which they do so will be the subject of this chapter.

Another movement called "Formalism" flourished in Russia in the twenties, and in many respects was similar to the Anglo-American criticism.[3] There are three parallels between the two movements.[4] First, both the New Critics and the Russian Formalists attacked the historical and philological scholarship that was current at the beginning of the century, and which dominated European academia at the time; second, both claimed that literature is a self-contained activity that should emphasize the autonomy of the text (that is, separating the poem from the poet, the reader, and environment); and third, both movements developed a method of textual analysis to replace the historical, philological, or moral approaches used to understand and talk about literature.[5]

The American Formalists (and here "Formalism" and "Formalists" are used in this chapter to refer to "New Criticism" and "New Critics" respectively) exercised a decisive influence on the American critical scene for almost two decades. One of their achievements was the emphasis placed on the words on the page, the meaning of the text itself as independent of its reader, author, and moment. Whereas the previous mode of literary analysis took the text as a point of departure toward understanding the psychology of the author, or the socioeconomic conditions of the time, the American Formalists directed their attention to the complexity and richness of the verbal construct. Although they never claimed that literature could be divorced from life, their preoccupation with the text marked a new trend of reading characterized by its emphasis on minute linguistic details and on verbal nuances.

We can better understand the New Critics' defense of literature if we place it within the tradition of "apologetics" or the "apology."[6] One of the concerns in critical theory has been to defend literature against the charges of immorality, uselessness, and triviality. Plato, for instance, attacks poetry on epistemological grounds; he disparages poetry and eventually rejects it from his *Republic* because it is an imitation of an imitation; a carpenter is more knowledgeable than a poet because the former's table is only once removed from reality, whereas the poet's is twice removed, and thus inferior. Plato also attacked poetry because it nourishes the passions. Aristotle's *Poetics* could be read as a defense against Plato's charges: Aristotle rejects Plato's notion of imitation, and builds instead a system of organic unity in which a thing tries to achieve its "thingness" (although Aristotle's notion of "thingness" is not identical with Plato's "idea," it is nevertheless similar to it). The cathartic doctrine has been interpreted as an answer to Plato's misgivings about nourishing the passions; for Aristotle "feeding and watering the passions" brings satisfaction and calm to the spectator.

Sir Philip Sidney, in a posthumously published essay entitled *An Apology for Poetry* (1595), also defends literature against the Puritans who claimed that it was "immoral, debilitating, lying, and provocative of debauchery."[7] Sidney dispenses with the Puritan objections by affirming that the poet invents a "golden world" of his own imagination that is superior and more beautiful than this "brazen world," and that the "poet nothing affirmeth, and therefore never lieth" because he works within the "zodiac" of his own imagination. Shelley's *Defence of Poetry* (1840) was written against the charges put forward by Thomas Love Peacock in *The Four Ages of Poetry* (1820) that "poetry has outlived its usefulness in an age of knowledge, reason, and enlightenment" and that it "appealed only to obscurantism and superstition."[8] Shelley's reply affirms the transcendence of poets, and he endows them with insights into "the eternal patterns that underlie all reality."

Matthew Arnold faced a similar charge against poetry in the second half of the nineteenth century, a time when science and technology were becoming increasingly more important. Science seemed like a panacea—the cure for all the woes and problems of the age. When Thomas Henry Huxley pronounced a "funeral oration" on literary education at the opening of a college, Arnold rejected Huxley's accusation that literature is merely *belles lettres;* Arnold averred that poetry (here he uses "poetry" to include all imaginative literature) reaches out and begins with all knowledge—political, social, scientific—and it is "the best which has been thought and said in the world."[9] Arnold found in poetry the substitute for religion:

> More and more mankind will discover that we have to turn to poetry to interpret life for us, to console us, to sustain us. Without poetry, our science will appear incomplete; and most of what now passes with us for religion and philosophy will be replaced by poetry.[10]

Arnold's didacticism is understandable if we take into account his defensive attitude. In fact, it is the attitude that all the "apologies" have in common. They are all passionate, didactic, inconsistent, and ultimately futile because they are essentially reactions rather than positive affirmations.

A. I. A. Richards

Like any other movement, neither the American Formalist Critics nor their assumptions can be understood without tracing the influences of the major figures that shaped or directed their practices. In fact, the two figures that directly influenced the American Formalists exerted such an effect on the movement that not only did their ideas and critical stands shape the ideas of the following generation, but also their very vocabulary permeated the jargon of the Formalists. I. A. Richards and T. S. Eliot are now generally accepted as the two major figures that influenced the American Formalists.[11] A basic understanding of both critics' stands is an essential corollary to any discussion of the Formalists.

Richards is of great importance to the development of American formalism and his use of the concept of catharsis is central to both his critical assumptions and to the critics whom he influenced. Confronted with the ideas of the Positivists and by their claim that literature has no value in a world dominated by science, Richards defends literature by relying on science itself, but Richards's science is a descriptive discipline, psychology. In his *Principles of Literary Criticism* (1925), he makes psychology a normative discipline through his theory of value. A person's life, according to Richards, is the astonishing metamorphosis of impulses, desires, and propensities, and of the never-ending process of their systematization by the individual. He believes a thing is valuable only insofar as "it satisfies an appetency," and the most valuable psychological state is that which satisfies the greatest number of appetencies with a minimum number of frustrations.[12]

Richards distinguishes between "ordinary experience" and "artistic experience," and it is no coincidence that to clarify both types of experiences, he cites the often-used example of the difference between witnessing a crime in real life and witnessing a crime in tragedy. The crime in real life is repulsive because the viewer is out of its context, because the viewer sees only a portion of the whole, and because the crime is blurred by details. The crime in a tragedy, however, is part of a whole, whose details the viewer is aware of; and because of mimesis, the crime is approximated to the viewer without the confusing details. The last experience is what Richards calls the artistic experience, and it is Richards's phrase for the cathartic experience, or in Joyce's terms, the static (aesthetic) experience, which brings into play the reconciliation of the greatest number of impulses.[13]

The crux of the problem of the function of literature and its relation to catharsis is this: is Richards merely alluding to Aristotle's "catharsis" or is he advancing a new and an independent theory of aesthetic response? The answer is that Richards's whole notion of "attitude," "experience," and "beauty" is nothing more than a rephrasing and reformulation of Aristotle's idea of catharsis. Richards defines the effect of art on its audience in the following manner: "It is in terms of attitudes, the resolutions, inter-animation, and balancing of impulses—*Aristotle's definition of Tragedy is an instance*—that all the most valuable effects of poetry must be described.[14] If Aristotle's meaning of catharsis has something to do with the reconciliation of pity and fear (for example, their purgation, clarification, expulsion), which is a reasonable traditional assumption, one could claim that Richards's aesthetic theory is nothing more than an expansion of Aristotle's cathartic principle.[15]

This is apparent even in his earlier writings. Richards wrote his first book, *The Foundations of Aesthetics* (1922), in collaboration with C. K. Ogden, a psychologist, and James Wood, an authority on art. In it, all three authors are concerned with the nature of "beauty." Their definition of beauty as that which is most conducive to synaesthetic equilibrium is curiously "cathartic." Beauty for Richards is in the recipient's mind, a state that comes after a long process of reconciling the discordant emotions that the work excites in the reader. Beauty in this sense is "relief," "reconciliation," or "poise." In their own way, Richards and his collaborators postulate the idea of beauty as an experience in the audience rather than an objective quality in the work of art itself. Their definition of equilibrium reinforces the cathartic principle even further: "In equilibrium, there is no tendency to action, and any concert-goer must have realized the impropriety of the view that action is the proper outcome of aesthetic appreciation.[16]

For Richards, to experience beauty is to experience synaesthesis, which is an aesthetic experience in which a harmony or equilibrium of impulses occurs. Richards's notion of equilibrium can be easily translated into James Joyce's "static emotion" where there is no desire to "go for" something and there is no active involvement, because to experience beauty is to have a feeling of "equanimity and freedom of spirit, united with the power and activity that a genuine work of art should leave us."[17] It is clear that even in his first book, Richards, by equating "beauty" with "relief," emphasizes the cathartic principle without using the word, disguising it under such psychologistic vocabulary as "synaesthesis" or "equilibrium." In his later works, he mainly elaborates his phraseology and refines his terms. The basic and essential idea of catharsis as conducive to the improvement of the reader through the regulation of his impulses will remain the same. It is Aristotle's catharsis, however we interpret the term.

Richards's *Principles of Literary Criticism* (1925) confirms his adherence to the principle of catharsis. His famous statement that poetry effects a "balance of reconciliation of opposite and discordant qualities" needs little explanation. According to Aristotle, among the emotions that are excited in tragedy are fear and pity, but they are not enough in themselves for the fulfillment of the tragic effect. Aristotle thinks these emotions should be governed by the rules of probability or necessity, a sort of tragic "decorum," to use a term that has fallen into disfavor in modern critical jargon. The tragic incident should involve a person who is like us, neither too low nor too high (the doctrine of mimesis). The hero, moreover, should be inflicted by a *hamartia*, a tragic flaw, which the

audience is privileged to perceive but of which the protagonist is unaware.

To further clarify Richards's position, let us backtrack a little. As
Aristotle explains in his *Rhetoric*, fear is an emotion we feel toward a
danger directed toward us (thus we might feel there is a possibility of
becoming like the protagonist, a victim), but pity is an emotion we feel
toward others, when we sympathize with their plight. Obviously, although we might imagine that we would feel fear if we were in the place
of another, the two emotions are essentially contradictory; they are "discordant," or "opposites," as Richards prefers to call them. The two emotions are united by a single element, and that is imagination, which fuses
the two into one by amalgamating two discordant qualities and making
them lead into a single action, which is catharsis: unless we, the audience,
make a logical leap from the action we perceive as possible outside ourselves (that is, in the art work itself) to the effects of the action inside
ourselves, the process of identification with the protagonist and the subsequent catharsis, which is brought about in the audience by the action,
would not occur. In other words, the process of witnessing a tragedy and
the elements of pity and fear, which are conducive to a tragedy's effects on
the audience, are in themselves two separate entities. One does not
essentially lead into the other. A third factor, a catalyst if you will, is
needed to approximate in the minds of the audience the particular experience presented in the tragedy, to bind together the feeling shown by the
audience and the action of the play on stage. This catalyst is the imagination. Referring to the poet's imagination, Richards says:

> Pity, the impulse to approach, and Terror, the impulse to retreat, are brought
> in Tragedy to a reconciliation which they find nowhere else, and with them
> who knows what other allied groups of equally discordant impulses. Their
> union is an ordered single response in the *catharsis* by which Tragedy is
> reconciled, whether Aristotle meant anything of this kind or not. This is the
> explanation of that sense of release, of repose in the midst of stress, of
> balance and composure, given to Tragedy, for there is no other way in which
> such impulses, once awakened, can be set at rest without suppression.[18]

Elsewhere, Richards emphasizes the "balancing of emotions" (p.
113). Whether this balance is achieved through the "union" of emotions or
their "organization" is of little importance. The salient point is that
Richards emphasizes their "reconciliation" as a prerequisite for catharsis,
or the "relief" we feel after we witness a tragedy. Richards discards the
confusing wording of Aristotle's translators, replacing their words with
psychological terms. Richards does not rely on the ambiguity of the words
"emotions" or "feelings," and the pitfalls inherent in distinguishing be-

tween the two (as Eliot will later try to do), but rather prefers the term
"impulses," which is more precise. Unfortunately, by using "impulse,"
which has direct psychological connotations, Richards found himself in an
indefensible position and vulnerable to charges of simplistic behaviorism
or "psychologism," a label that has become an effective weapon in the
hands of some critics to attack other approaches that do not conform to
their own specifications of what critics should do.

The next question is, how does Richards precisely understand
catharsis? Richards actually says that catharsis is the poise that comes
from the tragic experience:

> The joy which is so strangely the heart of the [tragic] experience is not an
> indication that 'all's right with the world' or that 'somewhere, somehow,
> there is Justice'; *it is an indication that all is right here and now in the
> nervous system.* Because Tragedy is the experience which most invites these
> subterfuges, [suppressions and subliminations employed to avoid unpleasant
> experiences], *it is the greatest and the rarest thing in literature.*[19]

Since tragedy is associated with the physical or spiritual defeat of the
hero, and since we identify with the hero, pain is inevitable. The spectator is faced with an unpleasant experience, which he comes to terms
with only when he resolves this crisis in his "nervous system" by reconciling the conflicting emotions.

The tragic experience makes us aware of two distinct emotions: fear
and pity. Richards contends elsewhere that when we see a tragedy these
two emotions are "painful" and "constricting." But the emotions that follow the cathartic experience, that is after we have reconciled the two
emotions through catharsis, are "emotions of expansion and release."[20]
What this statement amounts to is that, for Richards, catharsis is release
and liberation, liberation in the sense that catharsis relieves us from the
burden of ordinary emotions, since the emotions that follow catharsis, or
any other meaningful aesthetic experience, are quite different. Moreover,
they are not only different but, as Richards might have put it, also health-
ier for the nervous system.

Richards's preoccupation with synaesthesis and the notion of poetry
as the reconciliation of different impulses, leading to the "balanced
poise," has had two implications for the critics who followed him. The first
is that beauty is a subjective quality in the mind of the beholder, and in
his response to it rather than to an objective entity inherent in the work of
art itself. "The balance is not in the structure of the stimulating object, it
is in the response." The second implication is that catharsis as the reaction
to art brings discordant impulses into harmony and equilibrium that

eventually bring to the recipient of art not purgation or purification, but joy and poise. Both implications are of great consequence to contemporary critical theory, and they are of central concern to modern criticism. The cathartic principle as Richards uses and defines it turns into a sophisticated concept, on the one hand derived from and supported by psychology and on the other hand including tragedy, all literature, and even "a carpet or a pot."

Richards's explanation of catharsis in purely physiological terms as affecting the nervous system, however, disturbed many critics. Probably the most disturbing part was Richards's practice of talking about poetry (using the term once again in its general sense to refer to imaginative literature) in a vocabulary borrowed from other disciplines such as physiology and behavioristic psychology. He replaced a hazy, blurred language of criticism enveloped in metaphysical and mystical obfuscations by a more precise vocabulary. The use of this new language necessarily entailed a new way of looking at poetry, its effects, and its functions. His innovation in critical vocabulary entailed more than "changing hats," because the new language implied a new awareness, a new world view. Although one cannot ignore the limitations that often occur when criticism borrows the language of other disciplines, and the dangers inherent in transferring "alien" concepts to the analysis of poetry, the fact remains that the new vocabulary eventually enriches our scope of interest, widens our range of subject matter, and finally provides us with new weapons to attack old castles (to use a belligerent metaphor in keeping with the tone of Formalist writings). Terms as confused and misused as catharsis have been employed fruitlessly to a great extent, and so much ink has been spilt on the topic of catharsis that one wonders whether Richards's new views were really that alarming.

We can understand why a critic like Stanley E. Hyman is bewildered by Richards's versatility and his wide range of interests. Hyman would rather have Richards stick to one field:

> In *The Foundations of Aesthetics* he set up as an aesthetician, and in *The Meaning of Meaning* as an epistemologist and what he calls alternately a "symbologist" and a "semanticist." He has always been a psychologist, and calling himself a "centrist," has drawn enthusiastically and impartially on physiological and neurological psychology, behaviorism, Pavlov's conditioned-reflex psychology, psychoanalysis, Gestalt, and snips and snatches from almost every other psychological theorizer or experimenter, as well as on his own empirical observation.[21]

Hyman praises Richards for his knowledge, intelligence, and sensibility, but his not altogether suppressed annoyance at Richards's diverse interests is an attitude shared by many critics, who essentially express distrust or even fear at the introduction of new vocabulary into their "literary realms." One gets the impression that most of the critics who have written on Richards feel that he is an odd "insider" and wish he could be dispensed with as an "outsider."[22]

B. T. S. Eliot

The second major figure who influenced New Criticism is Eliot. His most important essay, "Tradition and the Individual Talent" (1917), is the key to all his later critical work. In it, Eliot states his basic critical assumptions and his fundamental concerns about poetry, how it functions, how it is created, its impersonality, and the meaning of "tradition." The essay had great influence on a generation of American Formalists, an influence buttressed by Eliot's status as a poet and critic. Two terms are crucial to Eliot's treatment of catharsis: "impersonality," and the "objective correlative." We need to understand them before we see how Eliot works catharsis into them.

Eliot understands "impersonality" as the poet's attempt to suppress his eccentric personality and unite his own particular experience with that of his culture. The poet's measure of success in this endeavor is the extent to which he has sacrificed his self, and the measure to which that sacrifice and surrender conform to that tradition: "What happens is a continual surrender of himself [the poet] as he is at the moment to something which is more valuable. The progress of an artist is a continual self-sacrifice, a continual extinction of personality."[23]

Eliot's critical thought reflects the cathartic principle in different ways. We have already noticed that the simplest way to understand catharsis is in terms of the effect of the poem on the reader. Another way critics have understood catharsis is the effect the writing of a poem has on the poet himself. The reciprocal relationship between reader/poem and poet/poem reflects not only the cathartic tension between the three elements but also embraces the concept of creativity. That is, a critic is interested in what goes on in the mind of the poet as he writes a poem, and then by extension the way the reader reacts to the poet through the poem. Eliot actually accepts both notions with qualifications.

Eliot makes an obscure distinction between "feeling" and "emotion" in "Tradition and the Individual Talent," which he does not maintain in his other writings. By "emotions" he implies something highly personal and vague; while by "feeling" he implies something distinct and precise, because it is attached to an object. However, in another essay, "Hamlet" (1919), we find that the "objective correlative" is a situation that contains

inherent "feelings" that express the poet's "emotions," and which stimu-
late similar "emotions" in the reader. The key phrase is "the poet's 'emotions,'" a phrase Eliot cannot avoid, despite his earlier assertion in "Tradition and the Individual Talent" that "Poetry is not a turning loose of
emotion, but an escape of emotion." As Northrop Frye asserts, Eliot
actually says a poet makes "emotion communicable to the reader" through
the objective correlative.[24] For Eliot, the essence of the cathartic notion in
the "objective correlative" is its ability to communicate the poet's suffering to his audience, or as René Wellek says, "Eliot introduces his theory
of catharsis . . . [as] the poet's self-purgation through art."[25]

There are other instances in Eliot where he expresses the self-
purgation of the poet. He uses a scientific analogy to define the poetic
process (which is cathartic since it expresses the tension between reader/
poet/poem) as analogous to what "takes place when a bit of finely filiated
platinum is introduced into a chamber containing oxygen and sulphur
dioxide" (p. 7). If the mind of the poet is that piece of platinum, and the
final product is the sulphuric acid, which is the poem, then the two gases
are emotion and feelings. But, then, Eliot immediately introduces a
strange notion about the suffering of the poet:

> The more perfect the artist, the more completely separate in him will be the
> man who suffers and the mind which creates, the more perfectly will the
> mind digest and transmute the passions which are its material.[26]

This is, plainly and simply, author-catharsis: the poet suffers, and to alleviate his feelings or emotions he transmutes his suffering into a poem.
The poem is, in Eliot's terms, the objective correlative of a particular
poet's suffering, and this in fact is the very concept of catharsis held by the
Romantics (as explained in the first section of chapter 1).

Despite Eliot's constant attempt in his criticism to exclude "emotions" from poetry in order to maintain the validity of the impersonal
theory or the "depersonalization of poetry," he cannot do so. "Emotions"
always find their way into his writings. S. E. Hyman observed this tendency and makes this comment: "Thus the emotion-feeling is a way of
barring "emotion" from poetry, in keeping with the impersonal and traditional theories, and then sneaking it back under another name and (perhaps) another form."[27]

Eliot's unsuccessful attempt to exclude emotions from poetry manifests itself in different aspects of his work and at different stages of his life.
He talks about his own use of emotion in remarks he made on *The Waste
Land*, for instance, a poem he wrote while undergoing deep personal and
mental suffering: "To me it was only the relief of a personal and wholly

insignificant grouse against life . . . just . . . a piece of rhythmical grumbling."[28] Eliot's adherence to catharsis manifests itself in the very way he phrases his sentence: first, writing the poem was fundamentally a personal experience; second, what initiated the writing was a suffering, a personal agony; and third, the writing itself gave him a sense of relief analogous to the relief of a disturbed boy listening to a nursery rhyme and repeating it to himself as mere "rhythmical grumbling."

No matter how hard we defend his objective and "impersonal" concepts of art, Eliot's critical writing, when taken as a whole, reflects a certain uneasiness, uncertainty, and even contradiction in his basic critical assumptions. Although at the heart of his criticism and his practice of poetry is the idea of catharsis, his earlier writings also show a noticeable tilt toward a serious consideration of the effect of a poem on the author. Eliot's constant emphasis on the impersonality of art is betrayed by passages that attribute catharsis to the poet's intimate personal suffering. Eliot has even affirmed, "We all have to choose whatever subject matter affords us the deepest and most secret release"—a sentence that beyond doubt derives its significance and meaning from both psychoanalysis and I. A. Richards.[29] Moreover, Eliot's emphasis on author-catharsis extends to such statements as the poet makes "into something rich" his most "personal and private agonies."[30] Eliot at one time even asserts that the function of criticism is nothing but the "pressing and pressing the essence of each author."[31]

Many critics have noted that Richards's ideas and vocabulary permeate Eliot's writings. For example, R. P. Blackmur argues that Richards's influence on Eliot is "not insignificant."[32] Eliot himself regretted his failure to benefit from Richards's criticism before publishing *The Use of Poetry and the Use of Criticism* (1933), because he could not get in touch with Richards before submitting the manuscript to the press.[33] Richards's emphasis and preoccupation with "emotions" as the key to the value of art had its repercussions on Eliot, who claims that the "enjoyment of poetry" derives from "a pure contemplation from which all accidents of personal emotion are removed." Eliot describes writing poetry as a compulsion: "the poet is tormented primarily by the need to write a poem."[34] Although Eliot makes such statements in seeming contradiction to Richards, Richards's influence extended to much subtler issues. When Eliot talks about ideas, which for him are one of the main sources of poetry, his vocabulary is colored by Richards's notion of the impulses and their physiological aspects. According to Eliot, "poetry can be penetrated by a philosophical idea, it can deal with this idea when it has reached the point of immediate acceptance [by the reader], when it has become almost a physical modification."[35] Oddly enough, the phrase "physical modification" ascribes the characteristics of physiological reactions on the reader's part to intellectual and philosophical ideas. For Eliot, the idea, taken by itself, is cool, detached, abstract, and almost meaningless; it is when the idea is communicated to the reader, when the idea manifests itself in the reader's physical sensations that it attains its value, warmth, and meaning. In short, when the reader's emotions are involved, poetry becomes communicable. If poetry does not excite the reader emotionally, then the philosophical ideas will be mere abstractions.

A similar cathartic notion occurs when Eliot censures Massinger, who, he says, is insufficient because he "dealt not with emotions so much as with the social abstractions of emotions. . . . He was not guided by direct communications through the nerves."[36] This passage sounds more like it was written by Richards than Eliot. For Eliot, the main criticism of value, here, is the "physiological sensation" experienced by the reader, which is quite reminiscent of Richards's "synaesthesis." Eliot censures Massinger because Massinger does not affect his readers to the extent that their reaction is visible in terms of "communications through the nerves." Eliot describes catharsis in purely physiological terms as affecting the nervous system.

Despite his emphasis on "impersonality" and objectivity, Eliot could not avoid talking about literature in cathartic terms. Sometimes, he thinks the writing itself brings a sense of relief; at other times, he says, the reader reacts to works of art physiologically; and finally he censures a poet's idea unless it performs some sort of catharsis on the reader in terms of "physical modification." Eliot could not isolate the literary text from its environment, from its reader and author. One of his most sympathetic readers, F. O. Matthiessen, defends Eliot against the charges of overintellectualizing, and says that Eliot

> has himself taken pains on many occasions to point out that the concern of the poet is never with thought so much as with finding "the emotional equivalent of thought"; that the essential function of poetry is not intellectual but emotional; that the business of Dante or Shakespeare was "to express the greatest emotional intensity of his time, based on whatever his time happened to think."[37]

At one point Eliot dismisses the objective criterion of poetry and acknowledges that literature is a "superior amusement," asserting that it "certainly has something to do with morals, and with religion, and even with politics perhaps, though we cannot say what."[38] Eliot, after his "conversion," was certain it had something to do with religion. For us, literature has a cathartic function, whether religious, psychological, or intellectual.

C. The New Critics

The term "New Criticism" is relatively new in critical terminology. It was used in Germany by the Schlegel brothers, and in Italy by Benedetto Croce; Joel Spingarn also uses the term in his book on Croce's views, entitled *The New Criticism* (1911). An anthology of later critical essays edited by E. B. Burgum was also entitled *The New Criticism* (1930). It was John Crowe Ransom, however, who seems to have established the term as referring to a specific kind of writer in *The New Criticism* (1941).[39] Ransom's book was neither a celebration of the movement nor a sympathetic treatment of the critics he dealt with: I. A. Richards and William Empson, T. S. Eliot, and Yvor Winters. The last chapter of the book, "Wanted: An Ontological Critic" was something of a literary manifesto against the critical practices current in the early decades of this century. It was specifically an attack on academic historical scholarship, literary historians, and "vulgar Marxist and literary sociologists."[40] The "old critics" ignored the literary text: instead the text derived its value from the light it shed on the author's life, the historical incidents of the time, or the economic conditions of a given period. The New Critics, despite their individual differences, emphasized the "ontology" or autonomy of the text against the positivist claim that literature is a "useless" endeavor, compared to the "usefulness" of science and technology. The New Critics' reply was simply to affirm the richness and the complexity of the poetic language and the poetic world, as if that were enough justification for its existence and usefulness.

The American Formalists were also on the defensive. We remember that Richards defends literature by relying on science, the very weapon by which it was attacked. For Richards, science functions as an intermediary in our transactions with reality, whereas poetry has a different function: poetry helps keep us in a mentally balanced condition, so that the reader becomes a more sensitive and more resourceful human being, capable through synaesthesis of coping with this world of conflicting impulses and ideas. Eliot, by insisting on the impersonality of poetry, tried to isolate literature from other disciplines to underscore its autonomy and self-sufficiency. According to Eliot, the "dissociation of sensibility" (the rift between "thought" and "feeling") occurred sometime in the seventeenth century when man became secular, skeptical, alienated, and industrialized. It was science that brought this rift, and we might infer from Eliot that to achieve a unified sensibility, we would have to abandon the frame of thought and way of looking at the world that underlie scientific thought and achievement.

Ransom, the leading theoretician of New Criticism in its early stages, attacks violently what he thinks of as science. For Ransom, science always reduces the world into types, and thus deprives the world of its richness and particularity through abstraction and the kind of interest that is scientific. To counterattack this "interest" (and the militaristic diction is in tune with the New Critics's vituperative language and mood when they deal with science), the critic should show "disinterest" and "humility," and never impose his abstractions on the text.[41] Ransom's warnings find their theoretical manifestations in Cleanth Brooks's famous essay, "The heresy of paraphrase," in which he attacks the reduction of the text to abstract propositions, or to any other external criteria. Brooks, too, attacks science for its reductionism, saying "Love is the aesthetic of sex, lust is the science."[42] Nor does Allen Tate think highly of science; he argues that "poetry is not quite different from science but in essence is opposed to science."[43] Tate, in fact, endows literature with the power to convey knowledge, saying, "literature conveys the special, unique, and complete knowledge."[44] Instances of such attacks and disparagements on and of science could be multiplied by further quotations from each of the New Critics. Implied in these attacks on science is the notion that literature is a no less valuable, essential, or even effective discipline than science. If literature could be shown to possess its own kind of knowledge, so the New Critics argued, then literature could justify its own existence.

It is both ironic and unfortunate that the New Critics' preoccupation with the "world's body" led eventually to divesting of its "body" the kind of poetry they were particularly interested in defending. The New Critics' readings and pursuit of minute linguistic details, as if the text (and its meaning) were only a verbal construct decoded or decodable by verbal manipulation, led to the kind of abstraction they attributed to science. That the New Critics were enemies of "science" or "positivism" is obvious, but what their meticulous verbal analyses amounted to was the isolation of the text from the reader, the author, and the moment—or from catharsis, in the general sense that we have been using the term. This is why opponents of New Criticism accuse "scientific empiricism," and objective interpretation of performing "a rape of the text."[45] Pushed to the extreme, the New Critics' treatment of texts as mere objects, rather than experiences, implied an assault on the text's relationship with the human condition. A contemporary critic has gone so far as to say: "The difference between seeing literature as an 'experience' rather than as an 'object' corresponds to the difference between treating human beings as *persons* rather than *things*."[46]

The New Critics were not, however, as "objective" and "impersonal" as their critics accuse them of being. By "New Critics" I am, here, referring to John Crowe Ransom, Yvor Winters, R. P. Blackmur, Allen

Tate, Cleanth Brooks, and William K. Wimsatt. I exclude Kenneth Burke and René Wellek from the list, although a critic like Richard Foster quite comfortably includes Wellek with "Brooks, Tate, Ransom, and Warren," and Wayne Booth has referred to both Wellek and Warren as "The Unnew Critics."[47] Burke's interests and critical practice are anything but Formalist. Wellek has been lumped with the New Critics mistakenly. What initiated his inclusion is, apparently, his influential study, with Austin Warren, entitled *Theory of Literature* (1942), which specifically draws a line between "intrinsic" and "extrinsic" aspects of literature. What is relevant to the text itself, or "the words on the page" is called "intrinsic," and what is relevant to the author, reader, or environment is "extrinsic." Of the critics on my list, although they share the idea that criticism should be intrinsic, Ransom, for instance, thinks poetry is paraphrasable, whereas Brooks does not. Other differences between the New Critics will be dealt with when we relate what they say to their historical context and to their attitudes toward catharsis.

Both Richards and Eliot, each in his own way, pay serious consideration to catharsis and its related critical problems: the role of the reader in the text, the effect of the poem on its creator and recreator, and the role poetry plays in our lives. One of the strategies their successors, the Formalists (or the New Critics), adopted to preclude the cathartic principle, to achieve objectivity, was to dismiss any reference to emotions and feelings, with respect to the reader and the author. This is actually where the core of their "objectivity" lies. Feelings and emotions are dismissed as mere "psychologisms." If it were possible for the New Critics to restrict their vocabulary to the text alone, then any reference to the reader or author becomes extrinsic, or peripheral.

Ransom's "ontology" is a tortuous way of talking about the intrinsic qualities of poetry. Like Eliot, Ransom tries to dismiss emotions; for him there is "no emotion at all until an object has furnished the occasion for one," because "emotions are correlatives of cognitive objects."[48] This is one version of Eliot's "objective correlative," although Eliot lacked Ransom's temerity in calling emotions the "correlatives of cognitive objects." Ransom first equates the aesthetic experience with the sentiment (the sentiment is obscurely distinguished from emotions and feelings), but then affirms that what is aesthetic is also essentially cognitive.[49] His obfuscating and evasive argument was one of the futile strategies adopted by some New Critics to avoid talking about "experience," the "reader," or "feelings." Even Ransom's meanderings and dodgings could not prevent him, however, from declaring that, "the human experience of the artwork is that it 'touches the heart.'"[50]

In Ransom's distinction between "structure" and "texture" in poetry, he inadvertently brings into focus the cathartic principle. For Ransom, "structure" refers to meaning, theme, or plot; in other words, it refers to the paraphrasable content of the poem. "Texture" refers to the poem's art, its sounds, its rhythm, and its images. As Richard Foster has rightly argued, structure corresponds to the intellect, which is a quality of prose, whereas texture is the psychological correspondence between the reader's feeling and all the qualities in the work that interest the reader aesthetically.[51] Actually, Ransom states categorically that texture, that is, "feelings," "is the thing that peculiarly qualifies a discourse as being poetic; it is its differentia."[52]

Ransom also claims that images and feelings are "Synonymous . . . insofar as they are one-to-one correspondents, one representing the cognitive side, and the other the affective side of the same experience."[53] The last phrase, "the affective side of the same experience" is at variance with Ransom's "ontology," that poetry has a complete independence in its own right. If he thinks that an image could represent cognition through the intellect and the affective at the same time, Ransom tacitly acknowledges the failure of his "ontology." Cognition represents the intellect, the ability to assimilate abstractions, while the affective side entails an emotional involvement. The fusion of the cognitive with the affective involves the concept of identification (the reader's identification with the text), where the emotional involvement requires the cognitive propensity of the reader to be able to transform a detached event into a personal thing, and this "internalization" of the event or action is not mechanical.

The contradictions apparent in Ransom's theory are not mere inconsistencies, but pitfalls inevitable in any literary theory that separates the text from its concomitant constituents: reader, creator, and environment. It is understandable why Ransom attacks in the strongest possible terms the concept of catharsis. Catharsis, even in its simplest meanings, unequivocally and blatantly refers to the effect of a text on its readers, and points to the tripartite relationship between poet/poem/reader. Ransom has to reject it, but he reveals his weakness by overstating his point. He relegates the term to the naive notion of therapy, and thus is capable not only of denouncing the concept but also equating it with regulated prostitution and other bugbears he despises:

> Catharsis was . . . a medical word adapted by Aristotle to the description of the effect of tragedy. It is a hard word for the lovers and respectors of art to have to come to. It reflects the patronizing view of certain natural scientists, who have strenuous programmes in view for humanity, and tolerate the arts only for medical or sanitary reasons, and in consideration for the present weak state of the racial mind. (In the same way we have seen systems of legalized and regulated prostitution, meant to take charge of an excess of

certain primitive energies; and systems of legalized and restricted liquor dispensaries.)[54]

When the New Critics attack catharsis, they systematically and intentionally reduce the concept to its simplest levels, namely, the morbid expulsion of emotions from a diseased body. This is why William K. Wimsatt says:

> My own view is that it is impossible for literary theory to make anything of *any* effective version of *Katharsis*, but that the theory itself is a harmless enough psychiatric appendage to Aristotle's actual literary theory. We can take it or leave it. And to leave it just as it stands . . . will be better.[55]

By dismissing catharsis from his critical theory, Wimsatt can concentrate his energies on the "words on the page," the verbal construct itself. He conceives the verbal construct "as existing somehow 'out there,' 'objectively' or at least hypostatized as an object and metaphorically as a spatial object."[56]

Wimsatt could not, however, ultimately banish the reader from his consideration. He has, in fact, referred to the reader as determining a certain kind of style, a certain kind of structure, and a certain kind of metaphor as if he were saying that style, structure, and metaphor exist somehow in the reader's mind rather than as mere verbal constructs "on the page," discerned or discernable only "objectively," as his theory advocates. An odd passage occurs in *The Verbal Icon* where Wimsatt claims that "at the fully cognitive level of appreciation we unite in our own minds both speakers and audience."[57] René Wellek has rightly observed that "Wimsatt seems to anticipate the 'fusion of horizons' proposed by the German advocates of *Rezeptionsästhetik*."[58] In other words, the notion of uniting "in our minds both speaker and audience" implies the concept of identification between creator (author) and recreator (reader) through a medium (text), which serves the vital role of unifying, approximating, or even identifying the experience of the reader with that of the author.

Yvor Winters was another New Critic who was never happy with the label "New Criticism" attached to his critical assumptions. Winters repeatedly criticizes Ransom for nominalism and hedonism, and he denies, unlike Ransom, that art is cognition. Winters expresses his doubts about Ransom's interpretation of catharsis, which emphasizes the medical purgation; and Winter's overall reading of the term (and not the concept) is tinged by uncertainty and uneasiness, reflecting deep skepticism of Ransom's interpretation of the term's "real" meaning:

> And it is characteristic of Ransom, that in his essay on Aristotle's cathartic principle, he should insist that Aristotle intended us to understand that

tragedy is merely a dose for getting rid of our emotions. He adduces in support of this view the fact that Aristotle was a physician; he fails to add that Aristotle, as a disciple of Plato, is comprehensible only within the Platonic context. I myself am incompetent to discuss the question of what Aristotle really meant, but if his meaning was the one that Ransom attributes to him, one can only regret it, for so great a man should have done better; the fact that Ransom can see no possibility of a better interpretation is characteristic of his awkwardness in writing of the function of poetry and of the manner in which his theories render poetry contemptible.[59]

Winters's allusion to a "better interpretation" of catharsis reflects an awareness of the possibility of alternatives other than the naive therapeutic reading, and his ironic skepticism reflects his contention that the concept is complex. He states his inability to deal with it competently, an ironic disparagement of Ransom's reductionism. He cautions against taking Ransom's therapeutic interpretation for granted, because Aristotle's discussion of catharsis, as well as of music, is "brief," "incomplete," and even "extremely contradictory." Winters thinks Aristotle contradicts himself, because he is either unaware of or disagrees with McKeon's division of the Aristotelian world of knowledge into domains, each domain having its own system, terminology, and interests. As was discussed in chapter 1, a consequence of such divisions is that what is said about catharsis in the *Politics* cannot apply to what is said about catharsis in the *Poetics.*

Winters's own critical doctrine is another version of the cathartic principle couched in different terminology. According to Winters: "The business of the poet can be stated simply. The poet deals with human experience in words. Words are symbols of concepts, which have acquired connotation of feeling in addition to their denotation of concept."[60] Poetry for Winters is, moreover, a rational statement having "a controlled content of feeling."[61] It is easy to follow Winters's argument because of his insistence on it, tirelessly and repeatedly: poetry is a rational statement having "a controlled content of feeling."[62] By "rational statement," Winters means that words are concepts that can be understood or rationalized; but words have, besides the conceptual aspect, a feeling-content value that the poet manipulates to adjust the concept to feeling, to bring forth feelings, attitudes, and judgments. Furthermore, Winters conceives of poetry as "a statement in words about a human experience." It is individualistic, feeling-oriented, and ultimately moral. In fact, Winters calls his critical approach moralistic "for lack of a better term."[63] The Renaissance view of catharsis as leading to moral improvement is basically echoed by Winters's reference to poetry as aiming to "increase the intelligence and strengthen the moral temper."[64] Catharsis, to put it slightly differently, is thus conducive to the strength of the moral judgment. Winters can formulate his cathartic doctrine because he endows words with the ability to communicate feelings. He says, "words communicate feelings by virtue of their conceptual identity."[65]

Another influential New Critic who "has been regarded as the American exemplar of the 'New Criticism'" is Cleanth Brooks; Wellek calls him "a critic of critics."[66] Brooks engages in "close reading," and he attaches great importance to such rhetorical devices as "paradox" and "irony." In fact, these devices become for Brooks the criteria by which a good poem is distinguished. Brooks's critical method has been directed relentlessly toward the following thesis: poetry is about nothing, and it cannot be paraphrased (because meaning is the paraphrasable part of the poem). We can define meaning only if we go "outside the poem." Literature for Brooks becomes a self-sustaining, self-sufficient entity ruled by its own structure, form, and logic. Literature is "about" nothing except the "perfection of its own intrinsic form."[67] Probably Brooks's most notable essay is "The Heresy of Paraphrase," which has become, along with Wimsatt and Beardsley's "The Affective Fallacy" and "The Intentional Fallacy," a catch phrase associated with New Criticism. The meaning of the poem should not be confused, according to Brooks, with external criteria, and thus the critic is discouraged from judging the "greatness" or "triviality" of poetry, since both involve the heresy of paraphrase.

Because Brooks is considered a representative figure of New Criticism, his method has been the subject of rigorous critical analyses and attacks. Gerald Graff, who attacks Brooks for his inconsistencies and contradictions, poses a central question: how could Brooks on the one hand attack "abstract philosophical yardsticks" because they appeal to the heresy of paraphrase, and on the other affirm that a good poem is "founded on facts of experience"? Graff's objection is thus centered on how Brooks can refer to ideas as "intrinsic" qualities in a work, and then judge them by referring to "extrinsic" standards. Graff argues:

> Clearly, to the degree that one judges poetry according to whether it is mature and founded on the facts of experience one is judging it no longer merely as speech in drama but as a kind of commentary, and the criteria of judgment cannot be called intrinsic.[68]

Brooks's insistence on the value of experience as the standard for judging poetry violates his notion of objectivity, because his standard relies on subjective, and hence external, criteria such as "intelligence," "mind," or "experience." Brooks has in other contexts conceded the fact that readers make out the meaning of a text (thus affirming implicitly that "the words on the page" do not in themselves have meaning).[69] On one occasion Brooks even refers to the different interpretations generated by a poem as fundamentally "reveal[ing] deep-seated cultural habits."[70]

Brooks acknowledges the importance of context, a somewhat disturbing notion for the New Critics because it is at variance with the notion of the "ontology" of the text. Brooks says: "I learned—in great part from him [i.e. from I. A. Richards], I think—of the importance of the context: that poetry was not a verbal bouquet of beautiful or exalted objects and ideas."[71] This passage might have been frowned on in the period when New Criticism was dominant, but now, after the movement has lost most of its enthusiastic drive and after so many attacks on its theory, the "critic of critics" makes some concessions by allowing different elements to interfere in the process of interpretation under the term "context." But Brooks's use of "context" is not that simple; he used "context" earlier in his career to mean something like the internal coherence or organicism of a work, a notion that was later developed by the contextualist critics.

Brooks writes about Yeats's themes: "Poetry yields a special kind of knowledge. Through poetry, man comes to know himself in relation to reality, and attains wisdom."[72] Wellek comments on this that "Brooks is defining his favorite poet's, Yeats's, view, but he could be speaking of his own."[73] For Brooks, poetry finally becomes flatly cathartic; it becomes conducive to self-awareness and wisdom. Just as Richards was able to speak of poetry as making a better human being, a more "balanced" person, so Brooks is able to define poetry in its relationship with reality and moral judgment. Brooks even asserts that the poet

> Must return to us the unity of the experience itself as man knows it in his own experience. The poem, if it be a true poem is a simulacrum of reality . . . by *being* an experience rather than any mere abstraction from experience.[74]

Brooks brings us back to where we started: a work of art to be valuable has to be related to human life and human experience. In short, it is valuable only in the context of its human "relatedness"; otherwise, a poem is not a simulacrum of reality, and thus it fails simply because it ignores the role of human values that regard literature, in the words of Cleanth Brooks, as "a portion of reality as viewed and valued by a human being. It is rendered coherent through a perspective of valuing."[75] According to Brooks, it is only the reader that imposes some sort of order derived from his values on the work of art to make it real, valuable, and even meaningful.

Because of their importance to critical theory, the concepts behind catharsis are manifest in the writings of the American Formalist critics even though the term catharsis rarely appears in their theoretical writings. As it appears in the writings of Ransom, Winters, or Wimsatt it is germane to a historical context, but treated as if it were a dead issue, of no use and relevance to modern critical thought. But the different concepts behind the term itself appear disguished under a different vocabulary. Richards, in talking about "synaesthesis," "beauty," and "poise," is actually referring to catharsis as it is popularly understood, as bringing harmony to the reader's physical being. Eliot, by emphasizing the impersonality of art, uses the "objective correlative" as an alternative to catharsis. Other Formalists tacitly acknowledge the concept of catharsis but use different terminology. Ransom, for instance, uses "structure," Winter uses "morality," and later on Eliseo Vivas will use "aesthetic transaction," and Murray Krieger will use, instead of catharsis, "transformation" or "revelation."

A persistent issue that occurs in the writings of the Formalists is that they all shirk catharsis. Why should they employ a different vocabulary to express the cathartic principle in alternative ways that are less exact? The reason is that the term "catharsis" has connotations for them that they think are overly simplistic and disparaging to the aesthetic experience. Bernays's influential study in Germany about catharsis established the medical connotations of the term, and thus they thought anyone mentioning catharsis was in reality talking about a relatively simplistic physiological aspect of literature. Second, Freud's usage of the term—a usage that was initially influenced by Bernays—further colored the term with therapeutic connotations. The fact that Freud considered the term an important part of his early career, and then discarded it because it described technically a therapy that was insufficient, made the Formalists think of catharsis only in therapeutic terms.

CHAPTER 5 Catharsis in Recent
Critical Theory

> When the emotional force, the mystic force one might
> say, of communication, of the miracle of shared life and
> shared experience is spontaneously felt, the hardness
> and crudeness of contemporary life will be bathed in the
> light that never was on land or sea.
>
> —JOHN DEWEY

THE INFLUENCE and pervasiveness of psychological criticism were from the beginning marred by abuses, reductionistic trends, and simplistic formulae. The critics who abused the insights of psychoanalysis on the nature of literary work, on human nature, and on literature as a cultural phenomenon, were critics whose conception of psychoanalysis was either based on popular notions of the discipline, or on an inadequate knowledge of Freud's writings. The reductionist aspect of psychological criticism lies in the way some critics treat different literary elements in the work of art, reducing them to fixed symbols, usually sexual. New Criticism, however, among other things, was a direct reaction to such psychological reduction, and the most representative pronouncement of New Critical doctrine that opposes the misuse of psychological criticism is "The Affective Fallacy," which is about the "confusion between the poem and its *results* (what it *is* and what it *does*)."[1] When New Criticism itself fell in the trap of reductionism by ignoring the psychological, historical, and cultural factors that shape literature and our understanding of it, then the multiplicity of contemporary critical schools emerged, filling the vacuum left by the New Criticism. The various critical approaches prevalent nowadays can be thought of as offshoots of either psychological criticism or New Criticism.

No movement has had so much influence on both modern critics and the classroom as New Criticism. It satisfied a need to return to the text, and the justification was simple: to understand a text, you have to read it closely and not rely for your understanding of it on psychological interpretations, sociological elements, or biographical traces. The study of what is related to the text is "intrinsic"; what is related to the author, the reader, or the environment is "extrinsic." The tenets of New Criticism, however, became institutionalized, and thus the movement lost the air and enthusiasm that accompanied its advent. Its basic premises became rules, and its preference of text over other considerations became doctrines. We associate the achievement of New Criticism with a method of reading, a method of teaching students how not to link "the words on the page" with psychological, biographical, and social considerations. Pushed to the extreme by the rigidity of pedagogical needs, the text became the sole criterion of interpretation. Because of the failure of the text to account for the explanation of different literary phenomena, the realization gradually came that New Criticism both as a critical method and as a critical theory was inadequate.

The collapse of New Criticism necessitated the emergence of a substitute critical school that would achieve what New Criticism could not do. The past twenty years or so have, therefore, witnessed a variety of new critical approaches and theories. The current situation in criticism is characterized by several qualities. One is its openness to borrow and use methods from linguistics, anthropology, psychology, philosophy, philosophy of science, history, the behavioral sciences, and even computer science. The notoriously short-lived school of French Structuralism, for example, conceived of establishing a science of criticism, a conception that ended with the French Structuralists recanting their ideas about structuralism and most of them becoming opponents of the movement.[2] Many have since adopted what has been called "poststructuralism," a critical school that some American critics refer to as "Deconstruction." If reference is made to the university where such critical practice thrives, then it is called "The Yale Deconstruction."

Modern critical thought is also characterized by a marked influence of different European schools of thought: French existentialism, German philosophy, and the ideas of the Prague Linguistic Circle.[3] Such openness to European thought is balanced by some American critics who have turned back to the methods of the New Criticism, further exploring them. Those critics have tended to mend the conceptual gaps in New Criticism's theoretical premises, and they have tried to suggest new ways of understanding New Criticism. The most outspoken adherents of the revitalization of New Criticism, or this neo-New Criticism, are, perhaps, Murray Krieger and Eliseo Vivas, and they refer to their critical practice as "contextualist criticism."

The deluge of "substitutes," other schools of criticism, to mend the inadequacy of the New Criticism has been characterized by polemics, a refusal to compromise, and short-lived critical schools. Reader-response criticism, a blanket term that indicates the concerns of the majority of modern critical practices, has concentrated on what New Criticism relegated to the background: the reader. The interest in the reader's response can be found in statements as early as Aristotle's catharsis, and we see it in Longinus's idea of transport; but at no time has the "reader" as a concept been subject to such scrupulous investigation as in reader-response criticism.[4]

Each of the five sections of this chapter will deal briefly with one or two critics from each of the five recent critical practices. Eliseo Vivas and Murray Krieger as the most outspoken adherents of "contextual criticism"; Northrop Frye, representing one approach within the various categories of structuralism; Norman Holland, representing the psychological trend in reader-response criticism; Wolfgang Iser, a phenomenological critic concerned with "text" and "reader"; and finally Hans Robert Jauss, representing the Aesthetics of Reception. One note of warning. The work of these critics is still incomplete, since all are still writing. I have chosen them because of the value of their contributions to the specific critical school they represent, and because of the depth of their insights into catharsis. It is a matter of debate how much any one critic represents the particular school under which he is classified, but my classification is by no means arbitrary. I have followed the general, accepted classification under which these critics are categorized.

A. The Contextualist Critics

The term "contextual" generally refers to the critic who sees the meaning of a literary work as determined by the totality of its surroundings, by its cultural environment, or by its psychological effects and insights. According to the contextualists, to apprehend a work of art is to endow it with cultural and personal determinants that different readers derive differently from the same text because each reader brings to the work his own peculiar determinants or concepts. In this way, the work becomes an expression of those determinants. In other words, we cannot isolate a work of art from its context. "Context" has been taken to be the cultural moment for the Marxists, a single structure in a monomyth for the archetypal critics, and so on. "Contextualism" in the wider sense thus refers to the practice of the critic who would place the work within a limited context, be it social, psychological, archetypal, or ideological. The interpretation of a work of art also depends on what constitutes the reader's "context"; indeed, one can understand what a given reading means or implies by referring to the context generated by the reader's mind.

In a more limited sense, "contextualism" refers to a group of critics who consider the verbal structure of a poem to be its own "context." Thus the narrow or technical meaning of contextualism is the opposite of what the term generally refers. Murray Krieger limited the term "contextualism," narrowing it down to refer to a specific critical "school" within the Formalists, in *The New Apologists for Poetry*. Elsewhere, Krieger refers to contextualism as "The name now commonly used to describe certain critical doctrines of the new criticism and of later theoretical developments made in sympathy with new critical attitudes."[5]

The contextual critics continue to develop the tenets of the New Criticism. One of the major concerns of the contextualists, for example, is the Richardsian dichotomy of the emotive-referential aspects of language. In his *Principles of Literary Criticism* (1925), I. A. Richards distinguishes between two uses of language: the first is that "a statement may be used for the sake of the *reference,* true or false, which it causes. This is the scientific use of language." Second, language may be "used for the effects in emotion and attitude produced by the reference it occasions. This is the *emotive* use of language."[6] According to Richards, the referential, or the first use, refers to a statement the truth of which can be verified by logic, and thus can be either "true" or "false." In the second use, poetic language is emotive in the sense that it does not make verifiable statements. The "pseudo-statements" of poetic language are cathartic since they appeal to emotions and attitudes and effect change in them. The scientific use of language is knowledge-seeking, whereas the poetic is emotion-seeking. For Richards, catharsis becomes the differentiae of poetry: if a discourse causes catharsis, then it is emotive; if not, then it is referential. In fact, Richards's catharsis partakes of both the emotional aspect of catharsis and its intellectual repercussions, since the ultimate aim of his version of catharsis is to regulate the conflicting impulses, and thus create a better person in terms of intellectual understanding and responses. In other words, the function of emotive language becomes, for Richards, the balancing of conflicting impulses; the referential, knowledge.

Cleanth Brooks, under Richards's influence, accepts the emotive-referential dichotomy, but he changes part of Richards's terminology. Richards's emotive use of language becomes the contextual, which for Brooks is solely determined by a dramatic structure emphasizing irony and paradox. Brooks's dichotomy becomes the referential-contextual. His contextual use of language is further governed by "the words on the page," and their capacity to generate new meanings through the tension that arises when "old" meanings clash with "new" meanings that a poem generates or suggests.[7]

The problem of the emotive-referential dichotomy haunts the later contextualists, such as Eliseo Vivas and Murray Krieger. Vivas expresses the problem in this way:

> How to explain the sense in which art embodies meanings which are not referential and are yet in some sense meaningful, and how to account for the mechanism by means of which it performs this feat, is a difficult problem which it is easy to overlook or brush aside.[8]

Murray Krieger, Vivas's pupil, states the problem in a similar way: "How can poetry tell us something about our world that we can learn nowhere else when for the contextualist it is not in any obvious sense referential?"[9]

The solution, for the contextualists, lies in the different functions words perform in poetry, as opposed to the way words function in scientific discourse. The words of a poem, being contextually controlled, interact with each other; they create their own "context." The old meanings struggle to suggest the new meaning that the poet intends. The tension created by the struggle between old meanings and new meanings is what distinguishes poetry from nonpoetry. The poet also struggles, as Krieger contends, to prevent the words from achieving their natural, referential function. Krieger uses "natural" to refer to the nonpoetic function.[10]

Walter Sutton attacked the contextualists in two articles appearing in 1958 and 1961.[11] Sutton argued that if a poem is self-contained and autonomous, as the contextualists claim, then it separates the reader's experience from the work of art. He points out, in other words, that the contextualists theoretically have fallaciously overlooked consideration of the cathartic principle. Therefore, this contextualism, which Hazard Adams hastily calls "an extension into theory of New Critical practice," could not stand alone, because critics can seal off from a literary work neither a reader's experience, nor other "cathartic" considerations, because what constitutes a "context" are the determinants that generate the meaning and not the words on the page alone.[12] Adams affirms that the contextualists actually end by reinforcing the cathartic principle: "In Vivas's view, it would seem that good art insists on making society know itself, while bad art . . . invites society to remain with its illusions."[13]

The contextualist critic actually sees the poet as clarifying or illuminating the human condition to his fellow human beings. This practice is far from the theoretical concerns of contextualism proper, or that extreme contextualism that shuns extrapoetic allusions. Besides, the contextual critic, in determining the aesthetics of a text, makes numerous references to the role of the reader, or the reader's experience. Thus Vivas acknowledges that the "intrinsic meanings of the poem derive from non aesthetic sources . . . [such as the] life lived by the poet who wrote the poem."[14] Once Vivas admits the importance of the reader and poet in determining meaning, the question arises as to what leads to the "aesthetic experience."

According to Vivas, art aims at arousing "an aesthetic experience of rapt attention which involves the intransitive apprehensions of an object's immanent meanings and values in their full presentational immediacy."[15] Vivas considers art to be "constitutive" of our world, and argues that art at once "creates" and "discovers" our values. According to Vivas, art is "constitutive" of reality rather than an imitation of it, but the difference between the two is tenuous, as pointed out by Vivas himself: "The reader may observe that I am pushing as far as I can a difference that I seem to have trouble making clear even to myself."[16] Vivas's confusion is apparent even when he tries to define some of his key terms, such as "intransitive" and "aesthetic experience," when one feels that he is at least alluding to the role of art as conducive to learning and to a better understanding of this world. As Adams says, "The definitions are distant cousins of Richards's balance of impulses."[17]

Vivas's concern and inclusion of extrinsic criteria to judge a work of art is apparent elsewhere. He says, for example: "Having read the novel intransitively, we can ask what the presuppositions are which must be posited as required to bring about and to sustain in the aesthetic transaction the work we have read."[18] The aesthetic experience, which he calls "the aesthetic transaction," cannot be an abstract contemplation; it is, rather, the interaction between the text and certain "presuppositions" of certain readers. What the statement amounts to saying, whether implicitly or explicitly, is that a given reader's "presuppositions" cannot be identical with every reader's presuppositions; or better still, "the words on the page" themselves are not a guarantee that the reader's interpretations, responses, or interactions with the text will be uniform. The same text generates different readings, because each reader has his own particular presuppositions or experiences.

Vivas asserts that the art work

> is ideal, in that its apprehension is rare, and that when we succeed in grasping it, it *brings with it rewards of a noble kind: peace, serenity, release from the sting of passion, and freedom from the indignity of living.*[19]

The ultimate end in Vivas's argument is that the text through enriching our experience will be able to make us better persons, more serene, more sympathetic, and more balanced physiologically and intellectually, because an art work both "releases" us from passions, and enables us to transcend "the indignity of living."

The same notion of catharsis is held by Krieger, who affirms that poetry will change its readers: "The contextualist will not forfeit the poem's chance to transform language—and its capacity to transform us."[20] The key phrase in Krieger's statement is the poem's "capacity to transform us." And this is how the idea of the autonomy of the text collapses, because the text's ultimate end is not its own existence, but rather its ability to change its readers, to perform some sort of catharsis. Krieger's notion of the transformation of the reader takes us back to Richards's conflicting impulses (via Vivas's "peace" and "serenity") and their final harmony. Krieger's concept of "transforming the reader" and his assertion elsewhere that "the ultimate function of a contextual poetry is to provide existential revelation" has broader implications than the work of Richards and Vivas.[21] For Richards, poetry primarily, although not solely, balances the conflicting impulses; for Vivas, poetry brings "serenity," "peace," and "transcendence." Krieger, under the influence of Vivas, extends the influence of poetry so that it becomes religious, intellectual, and psychological.[22] And this is where Krieger's catharsis lies. The ultimate end of poetry becomes a pragmatic process through which the reader is detached from his mundane and distracted reality into a realm dominantly, if not exclusively, aesthetic.[23] Supposedly, the reader is capable of achieving a state of transformation/revelation through a Coleridgean "suspension of disbelief" or identification with the text. The reader is capable of such transformation or revelation only if his own experience is somehow confronted, modified, or challenged by the text. It is only then that the reader's experience widens to include the author's. By the same token, it is this humane relationship that brings the creator and the recreator (the reader, because he recreates the work of art in his mind) together.

B. Structuralism

Structuralism refers to various critical activities primarily based on modern linguistic theory. The aim of such critical activity is to "construct a poetics which stands to literature as linguistics stands to language."[24] Within structuralism itself we can distinguish folk-and-myth oriented structuralism, linguistic structuralism per se, structuralist poetics, structuralist textual commentary, structuralist literary psychology, and semiology.[25] One of the basic premises in structuralism is that "the world is made up of relationships rather than things."[26] The consequence of underscoring *relationships* rather than *thingness* entails the primacy of the relationship over an entity; indeed, an entity or experience cannot be perceived unless its relationships with other entities or experiences of the same class of structure has been established.

The most influential work of structuralism in the English-speaking world is Northrop Frye's *Anatomy of Criticism* (1957), which Robert Scholes calls "a major document in Anglo-American Structuralism."[27] Frye tries in his *Anatomy* to start where Aristotle left off, but he recognizes that Aristotle's opening words in the *Poetics* "remain as good an introduction to the subject as ever, and describe the kind of approach that I have tried to keep in mind for myself."[28] Just as tragedy is a major topic in Aristotle's *Poetics,* so is tragedy in Frye's *Anatomy.* Frye identifies five modes and six phases of tragedy. The five modes refer to fictions that describe the hero's power of action as superior both to other men and to the environment down to action inferior in power to ourselves, that is, the antihero (pp. 33–34). The six phases of tragedy represent again a development of a world view starting with the heroic and ending with the ironic. We do not need to dwell on the complexity of Frye's typologies and classifications; they are irrelevant to our discussion of catharsis. For Frye, there are two views of literature that run throughout the history of literary criticism:

> These two views are the aesthetic and the creative, the Aristotelian and the Longinian, the view of literature as product and the view of literature as process. For Aristotle, the poem is a *techne* or aesthetic artifact: he is, as a critic, mainly interested in the more objective fictional forms, and his central conception is catharsis (p. 66).

Aristotle studies literature as a body of knowledge, and he divides it into parts, sections, and subdivisions; in short, he treats literature as an entity divisible into smaller units (plot, characters, and so forth). Frye, however, claims that catharsis is Aristotle's central conception. If we argue along Frye's lines, catharsis does not fit the Aristotelian objective categorizations. But Frye is apparently trying to compromise. He accepts Aristotle's *Poetics* as an objective, anatomical study, but then considers catharsis, the most unobjective aspect of the *Poetics,* to be Aristotle's central conception.[29] Such a contradiction in Frye's *Anatomy* cannot be resolved, and the contradiction leads to a series of other contradictions. For instance, Frye considers the *Peri Hupsous* (Longinus's *On the Sublime)* to express the concept of literature as *process,* whereas the Aristotelian *Poetics* expresses the concept of literature as a *product.* Although Frye does not explicitly say that catharsis expresses the view of literature as a product, his idea is that for Longinus transport or ecstasis holds a central position, just as catharsis is the concept central to Aristotle's *Poetics.* In such a system of priorities, we have two basic views: art as a process (Longinus) and art as a product (Aristotle). Put differently, there are two ways of looking at literature: literature as transport, and literature as catharsis.

There is considerable controversy concerning *On the Sublime (Peri Hupsous;* neither the date nor the author are, for example, known), but we need not delve into such controversies. For Longinus, or whoever wrote *Peri Hupsous,* the most basic conception of the sublime is the notion of transport. This is a *state* and not a *process,* because transport is essentially a description of what happens to the reader when he becomes so involved with the work of art that he is lifted out of his mundane, everyday life into a state of ecstasy. This state of ecstasy is transport. Transport becomes a process rather than a state when it is understood within the framework of catharsis. The cathartic experience begins with an emotional arousal, is followed by two contradictory emotions (often pity and fear), and concludes with their reconciliation. Transport enters the cathartic experience when the spectator identifies with the hero on the stage. In that particular moment, the play raises the spectator above the experiences of his everyday life and transports him to an aesthetic experience, what Lukács might call the transport from the generic to the specific. Such understanding of transport as a state within the *cathartic process* obliterates Frye's division of the two views of literature as either Longinian or Aristotelian (either transport or catharsis).

Another contradiction that Frye makes as a consequence of dividing the two views on literature as either Longinian or Aristotelian is his claim that "catharsis implies the detachment of the spectator, both from the work of art itself and from the author" (p. 67). Such a statement is self-defeating, since identification, not detachment, is an essential part of the cathartic process. Throughout the ages, identification has occupied different critics in different times, because without identification of some sort, the cathartic experience cannot take place.

Frye explains the traditional theory of catharsis, which emphasizes the "raising and casting out of emotions," as resulting in exhilaration or exuberance. In a passage that offers many insights into catharsis, Frye explains what he means:

> [Exuberance is] the vision of something liberated from experience into mimesis, of life into art, of routine into play. . . . The metaphor of creation suggests the parallel image of birth, the emergence of a new-born organism into independent life. The ecstasy of creation and its response produce . . . the sense of buoyancy or release that accompanies perfect discipline, when we no longer know the dancer from the dance (pp. 93–94).

Frye in the passage also expands the implications of catharsis and the cathartic experience through the use of his mythical system of death, rebirth, and ritual. The feeling of joy, or what Frye calls "exhilaration," or "exuberance," or "buoyancy," or "release," which he associates with the cathartic experience, is not a hedonistic or naive display of emotions by the spectator. It is a liberation of the individual from the particular experience that the work of art raises in him to a wider realm of reality, from private and personal worries to wider concerns. In short, Frye considers the feeling of catharsis as rebirth not of a new person but the rebirth of a new outlook that liberates us from our mundane concerns and leads us to an intellectually independent life. Frye goes so far as to claim that the sense of release associated with the cathartic experience brings forth a sense of complete harmony between the reader and the text, or as expressed in Yeats's words in the last line of "Among School Children" (1927): "How can we know the dancer from the dance?"

Frye's appeal to Yeats's last line is by no means perfunctory: Yeats expresses his view of life as a cosmic dance where all humanity becomes so involved in the dance that we cannot separate the dance from the dancer. The inseparability of the dance from the dancer in Yeats is related to his belief in rituals, rebirth, and order, a position with which Frye is quite sympathetic although both would define reality differently. The change in the reader's state of mind (the Greek word for state is *stasis*) can be detected here. For Frye, catharsis implies a change of status—when someone is born into or transformed into a new status through a cathartic experience.

The feeling of pleasure associated with art, which Frye calls "buoyancy," seems to him an inadequate description of the aesthetic feeling. He accepts William Blake's definition of beauty as exuberance, and says that it "seems to me a practically definitive solution, not only of the minor question of what beauty is, but of the far more important problem of what the conceptions of catharsis and ecstasis really mean" (p. 94).

Frye is the first critic in the history of literary theory to associate catharsis with ecstasis. Such an association provides a fruitful way of linking emotions (which basically come from ecstasis) with the intellect. The interaction of both results in the cathartic process. The association of emotions and intellect allows Frye to assert that "exuberance is, of course, as much intellectual as it is emotional" (p.94). For Frye, exuberance, which is associated with the cathartic experience, is a mark of imaginative power. In a passionate statement, Frye asserts: "The work of imagination presents us with a vision, not of personal greatness of the poet, but of something impersonal and far greater: the vision of a decisive act of spiritual freedom, the vision of the recreation of man" (p. 94). Vision, for Frye, finally results in spiritual liberation and rebirth, both of which are firmly based in our comprehension of beauty and of our exuberance—in short, in catharsis. Frye's defense of catharsis is perhaps the most passionate throughout the ages, because once the cathartic process is achieved, the spectator enjoys a sense of exuberance, which leads the spectator to envision change, creation, and sublimity.[30]

C. Reader-Response Criticism

The incessant questionings of New Criticism's premises and its opponents' vehement attacks against its theory and practices emphasized such concepts as "reader," "the reading process," and "response." Such emphasis naturally relegates to the background the author and the text. A new paradigm thus came into being that had the reader as its focal point. One of the consequences in the shift of the author-text paradigm to the reader-response paradigm is the change of the focus of literary study. According to Jane Tompkins, "As emphasis on the reader tends first to erode and then to destroy the objective text, there is an increasing effort on the part of the reader-oriented critic to redefine the aims and methods of literary study."[31]

One of the ways in which the redefinition of literary study has been directed is the concern with what constitutes the reader, the reading process, and the audience. Labels used to define the reader are legion: we have, to name a few, the real reader, the implied reader, the ideal reader, and the super reader. Another concern of the redefinition of literary study, the reading process, has been investigated less often, probably because of its comparative difficulty. It is easy to propose a label for a reader, and then quarrel about, modify, or compare similar labels. Another concern of the redefinition of literary study, the concept of audience, has received less attention than the reader or the reading process. Although "audience" and "reader" seem to be interchangeable terms, some critics try to differentiate between the two in their usage. One could say that whereas "reader" emphasizes the individual reader and reading as an individual experience, the concept of "audience" emphasizes a larger number of readers, sharing similar attitudes and concerns. The best study to date that investigates the different kinds of audiences is Peter Rabinowitz's four levels of audiences.[32] Similar to Rabinowitz's levels of audiences, but different in aim and focus, is Hans R. Jauss's "Levels of Identification of Hero with Audience," where the reader's involvement or engagement in the work of art is classified into five categories: associative identification, admiring identification, sympathetic identification, cathartic identification, and ironic identification.

Primary questions of reader-response criticism are: What constitutes meaning? Where does meaning lie? Is meaning in the text (that is, the words on the page), or in the reader? These questions have led to investigations, or, considering the polemics involved, quarrels. Parallel to the concern with the origin of meaning is the emphasis on meaning as "effect." Most of the reader-response critics define the "effects" of a text in terms of the meaning the reader gets from it. The argument runs along these lines: if meaning is the realization of the text in the reader's mind, then an accurate description of that meaning lies in its effects on the reader. Those "effects" can be investigated in terms of emotions, cognition, society, culture, and so forth. The study of literary effects is so wide and diverse that most classifications of the theoretical orientation of reader-response criticism include, according to one critic, such schools as "New Criticism [sic], structuralism, phenomenology, psychoanalysis, and deconstruction."[33]

Another critic labels almost all contemporary critical thought as reader-response criticism:

> We may distinguish . . . six varieties of (or approaches to) audience-oriented criticism: rhetorical; semiotic and structuralist; phenomenological; subjective and psychoanalytic; sociological and historical; and hermeneutic.[34]

The difficulty with such classification is that because the categories of a particular taxonomy are rigidly established or defined, the major categories eventually obliterate borderline cases. What such classifications basically imply is that the concern of reader-response criticism is as diverse as the concern of different, contemporary critical thought. Put differently, Susan Suleiman's classification implies that reader-response criticism is an ambiguous term that covers a wide variety of critical activity; which in turn means that there is no single critical approach that can rightly represent reader-response criticism.

Norman Holland's psychoanalytic writings, however, reflect the common concerns that preoccupy most, but not all, reader-response critics. Although I could have chosen another critic to represent the same concerns, Holland's critical activity, development, and interest in catharsis make him an acceptable candidate for one variety within the different interests of reader-response criticism. He considers that his critical development corresponds to the three phases of psychoanalysis: first, the opposition of the conscious versus the unconscious; second, the role of the ego in relation to the id and the superego, an idea developed by ego psychologists; and third, the concept of "identity theme," which reflects concern among contemporary psychoanalysts "who build a polarity between self and other rather than between ego and non-ego." Such a concern centers on the concept of identity as developed by two psychologists, Erik Erikson and Heinz Lichtenstein.[35]

Holland is heavily influenced by Simon Lesser, and he repeats Lesser on many occasions (as pointed out in our discussion of Simon Lesser). In *The Dynamics of Literary Response* (1968), for example, Holland claims that reading reduces the feelings of anxiety and guilt that people normally have in real life, which is a basic theme in Lesser's *Fiction and the Unconscious* (1957).[36] According to Holland, each literary text has at its core an unconscious fantasy. Such an unconscious fantasy is transformed into form and meaning. Just as Lesser emphasizes form and content as corresponding to defense and fantasy, so does Holland. Indeed, in *Dynamics*, Holland says, "Form in a literary work corresponds to defense; content to fantasy or impulse" (p. 131). The reader derives pleasure from reading because the work expresses his most primitive fantasies as the text contains the author's fantasies, which the reader in his turn discovers. The notion that books have or contain fantasies has dominated Holland's critical activity up a point. Holland claims that under the influence of David Bleich he discovered that books do not have fantasies, but people do.

This realization marks Holland's second phase of development, and its best representatives are *Poems in Persons* (1973) and *5 Readers Reading* (1975). Holland, however, does not change his views either on catharsis or on the aesthetic experience the reader gets from reading. Lesser's thesis remains the cornerstone of Holland's thinking. We find pleasure in confronting our fears in the works of fiction rather than in real life. Holland expresses Lesser's ideas in the following manner:

Each of us will find in the literary work the kind of thing we characteristically wish or fear the most. Therefore, to respond, we need to be able to recreate from the literary work our characteristic strategies for dealing with these deep wishes and fears.[37]

Holland alludes here to our involvement or engagement in the literary work. He emphasizes the individual pleasure we get from the work by emphasizing our hidden wishes, desires, fears, and impulses. He does not tell us about the quality of this engagement, but rather how it occurs. In short, Holland explains engagement or identification psychoanalytically by stressing wishes and fears as constituents of enjoyment. The leap from wishes and fears to enjoyment is not as abrupt as the passage suggests; elsewhere, Holland describes the transformation of fear into enjoyment:

Each reader, in effect, re-creates the work in terms of his own identity theme. First, he shapes it so it will pass through his adaptive and defensive strategies for coping with the world. Second, he re-creates from it the particular kind of fantasy and gratification he responds to. Finally, a third modality completes the individual's recreation of his identity or life-style from the literary work . . . . Thus we usually feel a need to transform raw fantasy into a total experience of esthetic, moral, intellectual, or social coherence and significance.[38]

According to Holland, each individual understands a literary work in his own way, because each one of us employs different strategies to understand the literary work, through which the work is filtered. The work itself appeals to our particular fears and fantasies. Finally, the total aesthetic experience gains aesthetic, moral, intellectual, or social significance depending on the reader's ability to transcend his raw fantasies.

Although Holland's contribution to the development of catharsis is minimal, his investigation into what constitutes meaning sheds some light on identification, a concept of prime importance for catharsis. The long passage quoted above, when looked at from a different perspective, shows how identification works. For Holland, the particular fantasy the text raises in the reader's mind makes the reader recreate the literary work, filtering it through his defenses and wishes. The particular gratification or catharsis that the reader derives from the work makes him recreate the work according to his own identity theme or life style.[39] The reader transforms his raw fantasy into different kinds of experiences according to his own identity theme; by extension, the emotional person will respond to a literary work emotionally, the intellectual intellectually, and so forth. Catharsis for Holland is not the end product of the reading process, but it

is one of its shaping forces. Although Holland does not address himself
specifically to the problems of catharsis or cathartic identification per se,
he shows some indications that it is one of his concerns. He affirms, for
instance, that "in the last analysis all art is . . . a comfort," a statement that
could be explained through the framework of the cathartic process.[40] The
cathartic process is always accompanied by a sense of relief that the reader
gets from the literary work. This relief Holland refers to as "comfort."

Holland's evasive treatment of catharsis in his early career leads him
to discuss how a painful experience can lead to pleasure, a phenomenon
he links, surprisingly, to mimesis rather than to catharsis:

> Neither Aristotle nor Arnold had a psychology adequate to the problem [of
> how a painful experience could be pleasurable], but the insights of both are
> sound, as far as they go. Translated into modern terms, they are describing
> our fourth pattern: painful events can given pleasure in tragedy because the
> work of art provides defensive ways of escaping the pain and somehow
> turning it into meaningful pleasure. Aristotle, typically Greek, stresses intel-
> lectualization as a defense. Arnold, typically Victorian, stresses action.[41]

There are many problems with Holland's statement. For instance, he does
not explain how the painful experience becomes pleasurable, except by
saying that "somehow" this pain is turned into pleasure. He leaves his
"somehow" ambiguous. The second problem is how Aristotle's notion of
pleasure coming from pain could be "intellectualization." Holland does
not justify the statement, nor does he explain how it occurs. Most disturbing of all, perhaps, is Holland's reductionistic treatment of art. He reduces
literature and literary phenomena (pleasure, pain, mimesis, catharsis) to
defenses. In fact, the only way in which Holland conceives of art is the
way it raises, confronts, or appeases our defenses and fears. Elsewhere,
however, Holland offers a traditional Freudian interpretation of catharsis
when he discusses the similarity between literature and play. In play, a
person "recreates" what disturbs him; the same process is involved in
literature. Holland argues,

> When literature "pleases," it, too, lets us experience a disturbance, then
> master it, but the disturbance is a fantasy rather than an event or activity.
> This pattern of disturbance and mastery distinguishes our pleasures in play
> and literature from simple sensuous pleasures.[42]

By saying that the pleasure we derive from a literary work comes
from "recreation" and "mastery," we see a revised version of the Freudian
formula of art as self-expression and self-mastery, only this time it is an art
that is mitigated by its being a mere fantasy. Holland draws a line be-

tween event, activity, and fantasy, and since he regards our reaction to art as fantasy rather than action it is hard to defend his trivialization of literature. Apparently, Holland is oblivious to the fact that in order for a reader to express himself, and then to be able to exercise some mastery over his feelings, he is not involved in a mere fantasy or a mild disturbance, but in an activity that is meaningful to him.

In summary, according to Holland, the patterns of disturbance and mastery that a work of art bring to us result in relief and comfort. Such feelings of relief and comfort are apparently emotional, but in our attempt to control or understand them, we raise them to the intellectual plane. The interplay of emotions and intellect makes the pleasure we derive from reading literature much more complicated than simple sensuous stimulation. Simple sensuous pleasure is one-sided (that is, it comes from real situations and not from vicarious aesthetic reactions) because it does not involve conflict; but the pleasure we derive from literature is complex because, first, it involves a conflict, and then it is intensified by "mimesis," the way an experience or an event is perceived vicariously by a reader or an audience. The pleasure we derive from real-life situations is mixed and blurred by other elements, but in literature, primarily owing to mimesis, all the frills are eliminated, and the pleasure becomes more intense, purer, and clearer. For instance, the simple sensuous pleasure in real life is blurred by ordinary concerns and daily problems, which finally mitigate our enjoyment. In art, we are moved to a different context, a context whose whole purpose is to make our pleasure undivided and unmitigated by other concerns.

D. Phenomenology

Since no satisfactory dictionary definition of phenomenology is available, a brief introduction will help our understanding of the phenomenology of Wolfgang Iser. Of the critical schools dealt with in this chapter, the oldest is phenomenology. It was established by the German philosopher Edmund Husserl (1859–1938), who undertook to describe consciousness as objectively as possible. For Husserl, consciousness is "intentional"; that is, it is directed toward an object. Husserl's ideas found many followers in different countries, such as Martin Heidegger in Germany, Roman Ingarden in Poland, and Maurice Merleau-Ponty in France. It was Ingarden (1893–1970), however, who tried perhaps more systematically than any other critic to account for the literary experience in a literary work through phenomenology. For Ingarden, a literary work originates in its author's intentional acts, acts that are directed toward an object. The intentional acts of the text allow the reader to reexperience the work in his own way.

For Iser, the reader reexperiences the work in his individual and unique way because each text contains "gaps of indeterminancy," which each reader, and even succeeding generations of readers, can fill differently. Every new reading of the same text by the same reader entails the discovery of new "gaps." To arrive at the meaning of a text, each reader fills in these gaps in his own way. The realization or concretization of the work is the way a reader responds to these gaps and the way he arrives at a particular meaning from his particular reading.

We associate Iser's name with the term "the implied reader," which is also the name of his first book.[43] In it, Iser analyzes ten novels; these analyses, arranged chronologically, illustrate "the succession of activities which the novel, from Bunyan to Beckett, has demanded from its readers." In his study of individual texts, Iser emphasizes the ways in which gaps or "spots of indeterminancy" operate, either by frustrating the reader's expectations or by encouraging him to transcend the text itself: that is, the reader gains insight into his own condition. Iser attempts to explain the interaction between "reader" and "text," or more specifically how the reader "realizes" the text in the reading process. This is why Iser talks about the reader's strategy and the text's "gaps" or "repertoire."[44] The "realization" of the text is the interaction between the reader's strategies and the gaps of the text. In his second book, *The Act of Reading,* Iser studies the theoretical problems involved in the reading process by relying on semiotics, communications theory, and experimental psychology.[45] But Iser avoids talking about catharsis in both books.[46] In fact, he uses the phrase "cathartic effect" only once in all his works translated into English, and it is interesting to discuss the term in that particular context. In *The Act of Reading,* Iser discusses a theoretical situation in texts where there is a conflict both internally, created by the characters themselves in a narrative, and externally, created by the reader when he tries to reconcile the inconsistencies in the text:

> The conflict itself arises when the reader tries to project one perspective [that is, "the narrator, the hero, the minor characters, or all the characters together"] onto another and finds himself confronted with inconsistencies; the solution to the conflict lies in some idea of reconciliation which is not formulated by the text (p. 47).

A basic component of Iser's concept of catharsis is the existence of conflicting elements in the work of art: evil and good, or sin and virtue, or fear and pity. These conflicting elements are in the work of art, but the

conflict should be internalized by the spectator. The reader's activity
becomes apparent only when he tries to reconcile these opposing forces
or conflicting elements. And this is what Iser is alluding to by emphasizing the three components of catharsis: first, the reader faces contradictory
elements (in the text itself); second, the solution of the conflict between
the elements lies in their reconciliation; and third, it is the reader who
resolves the conflict through his imagination, or as Iser says, "The reader
must work it out for himself if he is to make the experience his own"
(*AOR*, p. 48).

Iser compares such activity of reconciliation with the kind of texts
that do not give rise to such conflict, such as *romans à thèse*. These,
Iser contends, offer their own solutions, and so he dismisses them because "they serve a purely rhetorical function." Immediately after this
comment, Iser's reference to catharsis occurs:

> Only if the reader is involved in working out this solution, can there be a
> truly cathartic effect, for only participation—as opposed to mere contempla-
> tion—can bring the reader the hoped-for satisfaction, although Lesser and
> Richards would have you think otherwise (*AOR*, p. 48).

This passage is important in many ways, and it needs careful analysis,
because Iser bases his theory of aesthetic response on its underlying
assumptions. These four assumptions are as follows:

1. Iser's concern with the reading process as the interaction between
reader and text can be seen in terms of conflict: the reader's "strategy"
conflicts with the "repertoire" of the text. Such interaction creates tension. This tension is reconciled in the reader's transcendence of such
tension or conflict. Put differently, Iser confirms his adherence to catharsis: the conflict between the reader (spectator, recipient, addressee) and
the text (the book, the stage, the picture) is resolved in some reconciliation that makes the reader capable of detaching himself from the text and
looking critically at his human condition, what Iser calls "transcending the
text."

2. Iser agrees with Jauss's interpretation of catharsis as the emotional involvement or engagement of the spectator with the hero, although Jauss argues for catharsis as the first step in contemplation. On the
other hand, Iser's emphasis on detachment seems to contradict his previous statement on emotional involvement. But this is a superficial contradiction since emotional involvement eventually ends in contemplation, in
which the spectator begins to "transcend the text," and thus gains a better
understanding of himself.

3. Both Lesser and Richards were concerned with the implications of emotional involvement in the cathartic process. Lesser explains this involvement in psychoanalytic terms as satisfying some innate drives and fantasies, such as wish-fulfillment. But it seems that Iser misreads Richards. Richards's concern is not so much with the balance of conflicting emotions as it is with the idea that the catharsis brought by this harmony improves the reader's outlook and condition in this world. This position is not far from Iser's, especially when he argues that the text "activates our own faculties," and thus assumes the corrective attitude adopted by Richards that the text is supposed to improve the reader's self, soul, and human condition.[47]

4. Although Iser avoids talking about catharsis, the cathartic principle itself permeates most of his discussions. Thus he affirms that "meaning must ultimately resolve the tensions and conflict brought about by the text"; or that "we become aware that meaning . . . [is] a relief from tension" (AOR, p. 223).

Thus, Iser's approach is to a large extent heavily dependent on the cathartic principle, and if we take the main mark of catharsis to be the effect of the work of art on the reader, then we can associate Iser's position with catharsis. In fact, Iser affirms such closeness by saying:

> If the reader and the literary text are partners in a process of communication, and if what is communicated is to be of any value, our primary concern will no longer be the *meaning* of that text . . . but its *effect.* Herein lies the function of literature, and herein lies the justification for approaching literature from a functionalist standpoint (AOR, p. 54; Iser's emphasis).

In fact, Iser's whole notion of meaning is nothing but the effect of the work of art on its reader. He says, "Meaning is no longer an object to be defined, but is an effect to be experienced" (p. 10). Although Iser tries to distinguish between "meaning" as the referential totality of the text, and "significance" as the reader's internalization of the text into his experience (AOR, pp. 150–151), Iser ends up ignoring his distinction by affirming that meaning is an effect to be experienced. If meaning is effect, then that meaning is psyche-oriented and not text-oriented. The work of art helps us realize what is hidden within ourselves, and by bringing meaning to the surface, we bring our own memories, emotions, fantasies, fears, anxieties, and worries to the surface too. The result is that Iser's notion of catharsis takes us back to Lesser where we confront fears and anxieties in real life. But Iser goes beyond Lesser by emphasizing our "transcendence." That is, after we confront our memories, emotions, and anxieties, we begin to detach ourselves from those fears and thus gain an insight into their causes, our weaknesses, and our human condition.

E. Aesthetics of Reception

Parallel to the recent Anglo-American interest in the reader is the German *Rezeptionsästhetik*, the "aesthetics of reception" movement. It would be an oversimplification "to speak of one discipline" concerned with the study of reception because "'reception' comprises a number of research areas, each with its own method and epistemological framework."[48] It is, therefore, more practical to study the way one influential literary critic of this school understands and develops the term catharsis. Hans Robert Jauss is considered the leading theoretician of the aesthetics of reception, and he himself represents the complexity and diversity of the reception movement.[49] Unfortunately, my study ignores the study of reception in the German Democratic Republic, where critics have tried to compromise Marxist theory with reception, a position not too alien to Jauss himself.[50]

According to Rien Segers, "*Rezeptionsästhetik* (the aesthetics of reception) was introduced to Western Germany in the late sixties by Hans Robert Jauss."[51] The study of reception was a reaction to Marxist criticism and to historicism: the recipient has become a focus of literary research, and reception a criterion of literariness. The study of reception differs from historicism "in its renunciation of value-free research"[52] A Marxist looks at art-work as production, and consumption determines production in two ways: first, consumption makes the product a useful object, or as Marx says, "a garment becomes a real garment only through the act of being worn."[53] Similarly, a text becomes a text only when it is read. Second, production determines consumption in the sense that production determines both the means of consumption and the consumer. More important than the Marxist jargon, however, is the fact that the theoreticians of response talk about the dialectical relationship between consumer and product (text and reader), and production and reception.[54] Structuralism, especially in its emphasis on *relations* rather than *origins*, also influenced the study of response: a phenomenon cannot be studied in isolation but only through the relations it contains. The influence of the Prague Structuralists, or "dynamic structuralism," is also apparent in such formulations as the following by Mukařovský: "The literary work of art manifests itself as sign in its inner structure, in its relation to reality, and also in its relation to society, to its creator and its recipients."[55] The emphasis on text, society, and recipient is no more evident than in the writings of Jauss.

Jauss's name has been associated with his call for a new literary history based on reception.[56] In fact, a recent study treats the aesthetics of reception in Jauss's terms, formulating a new literary history.[57] Such a literary history is based on the assumption that art (in the general sense of the word that means imaginative literature) arises from historical and social functions. A corollary to this is another idea: "The work does not exist without its effect; its effect presupposes reception, and in turn the audience's production."[58]

The study of reception, Jauss contends, must begin with the relationship between the reader and the text. Meaning is not restricted to the text, but it is the reader's "concretization" of meaning, or what Jauss calls the fusion of two horizons: the first horizon is a social one, and it is provided by the text; the second is supplied by the reader (p. 141). Such fusion of horizons produces meaning, the purpose of which is catharsis, although the term itself is not used: "The relief from the restraint and monotony of everyday life, in the acceptance of an invitation to identify with a model, or more generally in the enrichment of a new or widened experience" (p. 141). Jauss considers the reader's "horizon of expectations" a "hermeneutic instrument," which the reader uses to arrive at the meaning of a text through the questions raised by his horizon of expectations.

Jauss traces the roots of receptional aesthetics in Aristotle's doctrine of catharsis, which he views as "historically the most fruitful approach for developing the problem of identification between hero and spectator."[59] A significant modification of the Aristotelian concept occurs when Jauss considers catharsis the decisive factor that transforms the "aesthetic experience into a symbolic or communicative action." (p. 285). Such an extension of catharsis as communication (for example, communication of morals, ideas, and values) allows Jauss to affirm that catharsis is "always a liberation *from* something as well as a liberation *for* something" (p. 288; Jauss's emphasis).

The dilemma of identification or the problem of how a spectator can approximate what he sees externally on the stage to what he feels internally is neatly resolved by Jauss:

> One's disposition to enjoy an aesthetic object presupposes the negation of everyday life. The acting subject must first become a spectator, listener, viewer, or reader in order to achieve that attitude of disinterested approval which enables him to reify the object of aesthetic awareness and so allows

him to identify himself with what is being presented, or with the hero (p. 286).⁶⁰

Jauss makes a clear distinction between "catharsis" and "everyday life," or, better still, between the "cathartic experience" and "everyday life experience." To emphasize the difference between the two experiences, Jauss considers the cathartic experience to be the "antithesis to the practical business of life." Moreover, Jauss considers catharsis as communication, a notion that allows him to attribute social functions to it, by saying that the cathartic experience either "passes on traditional patterns of behavior or creates new ones" or "introduces norms of behavior for the purpose of calling them into question or destroying them."

Jauss's use of catharsis is highly original, and he regards it as "the enjoyment of affects as stirred by speech or poetry which can bring about both a change in belief and the liberation of his mind [sic] in the reader or spectator."⁶¹ The cathartic experience presupposes aesthetic distance on the part of the spectator, because catharsis necessarily entails "a negation of the immediate interests of his [that is, the spectator's] everyday life" (p. 286). Since the experience we call catharsis presupposes some kind of identification on the part of the reader/spectator with the hero, the reader must detach himself from everyday life in order to experience what Jauss calls the "cathartic liberation."

Jauss's original understanding of catharsis is by no means restricted to its Aristotelian context; in fact, he explains it as follows:

> The classical model of catharsis includes the primary achievement of aesthetic experience: the liberation of the spectator from the objective world by means of the imaginary, which in turn constitutes the common ground of our delight in the tragic or comic (p. 286).

For Jauss, our enjoyment of the tragic or the comic includes our ability to be liberated from the objective world through the imaginary. Such a consideration of catharsis is aesthetic, because for Jauss cathartic identification can provide the observer with individual satisfaction in his liberation from everyday life, or this liberation can "induce him to be content with the mere pleasure of looking on."

Jauss views catharsis as fulfilling three basic functions (as shown in the outline on the following page): moral, social, aesthetic. These functions are contingent on the spectator's identification with the hero. This scheme, although reduced substantially for the sake of clarity, indicates to what extent Jauss is concerned with catharsis and the cathartic process as a unique phenomenon with repercussions that are social, moral, and aesthetic. Jauss attributes all these functions to catharsis be-

Moral and   A. emotional identification can pass on traditional pat-
Social   terns of behavior, or
Functions   B. create new ones, or
               C. introduce norms of behavior for negative purposes:
                    1. calling them into question, or
                    2. destroying them.

Aesthetic   A. Cathartic identification leads to "liberation."
Functions   1. It provides the observer with pure individual
                       satisfaction in his own liberation (liberation in the
                       sense that the spectator negates or suspends the
                       immediate interests of his everyday life), or,
                    2. it induces him to be content with the mere plea-
                       sure of looking on.
               B. The spectator who is liberated by the "pleasure in a
                  tragic object" can
                    1. assimilate what is exemplary in the action, or
                    2. refuse to enter in this identification, or
                    3. neutralize his identification or experience ethic-
                       ally by not going beyond a naive astonishment at
                       the deeds of the hero (p. 89).

cause he endows catharsis with a communicative value in the literary
experience. The author communicates his values, ideas, and the social
norms he believes in to the reader, who, in turn, receives these ideas
through identification, which finally leads to catharsis.

Although Jauss draws a line between *admiring* identification and
sympathetic identification, he is concerned with cathartic identification,
which "bring[s] about for him [i.e., the spectator] an inner liberation
which is supposed to facilitate the free use of his judgment rather than the
adoption of specific patterns of activity" (p. 297). When the spectator
refuses cathartic identification, that is when he refuses to be drawn into
the action of the play, or refuses to be "morally liberated" and is instead
content with the enjoyable identification by "succumb[ing] to the magical
power of illusion," however, then the spectator's refusal is called, according to Jauss, "ironic identification." For Jauss, the first type of
identification, the "cathartic," is positive because it is socially norm-
fulfilling in the sense that the spectator follows a model or imitates him.

The second type of identification, the "ironic," is norm-breaking in the sense that the spectator refuses to identify with the hero.

Since Jauss emphasizes identification as the key to the understanding of catharsis, a study in some detail of this concept will help us follow his thought. Jauss divides identification into five levels: associative, admiring, sympathetic, cathartic, and ironic.

1. Associative Identification.

By "associative identification" Jauss refers to a sort of aesthetic conduct in which the spectator assumes a role in the imaginary world of a play-action (p. 299). The emphasis here is on the suspension of the "opposition between presentation and contemplation, between actors and spectators," and the concept is derived from play-action, where the spectator participates in a game. The implications of games are of special interest to Jauss, because games play a "constructive role" in social groups. The social groups help the spectator/player develop his own identity and thus establish "modes of communication" (p. 300).

Jauss's reliance on game theory inadvertently trivializes literature: literature is a much more complex phenomenon than play and games and it is more serious. Only a positivist like Jeremy Bentham thought that poetry was as valuable as push-pin, or even less valuable since "anybody can play at push-pin: poetry and music are relished only by a few."[62] Although Jauss is influenced by Freud's concept of play, where the child abreacts his emotions and thus gains mastery of the situation, he does not elaborate his ideas on play.

Moreover, Jauss's terminology seems to be inaccurate: an alternative to Jauss's "associative" would be the "sublime identification," the notion of the sublime would precisely point to the aesthetic state in which the reader/addressee/recipient is lifted out of his daily concerns, and is mentally immersed in the action of the play, or the poem, or the text. The concept of the sublime, like catharsis, has been unnecessarily relegated to its mere Longinian context by modern critics. Identification where the spectator is lifted out of his mundane concerns and then is mentally involved in the action of the play should be explained within the concept of sublimity, which is at once more relevant and precise as far as literary theory is concerned.

2. Admiring Identification.

The aesthetic experience that is called admiring identification is related to the feeling of astonishment or admiration that the spectator feels toward a model. Such identification is directed toward the "manner in which models are fashioned and with their efficacy" (p. 303).

Jauss's concern with the social aspect of art is evident here too. The model, be it a hero, a situation, or an incident, is socially norm-fulfilling in the sense that the spectator should emulate it. This emulation, which is admiring identification, is an aesthetic experience. Such an experience "consolidate[s] experience of history and pass[es] it on from generation to generation" (p. 304). The essence of this aesthetic experience becomes an archetype—in the Jungian sense—of which whole groups are unaware.

3. Sympathetic Identification.

Sympathetic identification refers to the "aesthetic disposition" that transcends admiration and self-satisfaction and drives the spectator to action. Unlike the admiring identification, which centers on norm-centering "models," the sympathetic identification is centered on an "imperfect model," one who is close to being an everyday hero, and recognizable to the spectator through his mundane actions and quotidian qualities. Such identification can provide the spectator "with practical insight by way of moral identification" (p. 307).

4. Cathartic Identification.

Cathartic identification refers to the aesthetic state in which the spectator is "lifted out of the real interests . . . of his usual world and placed in the position of the suffering or hard-pressed hero in order to undergo, by comic release, an inner liberation" from the concerns of everyday life (p. 310). For Jauss, catharsis is not restricted to what is tragic, but it includes the comic effects of art, which he calls "release." Moreover, catharsis for Jauss is essentially a moral disposition arrived at through an aesthetic experience (p. 311).

Jauss thinks that cathartic identification emancipates the aesthetic experience by putting the spectator into a "level of critical reflection concerning what is presented." In other words, catharsis represents the shift from identification to reflection (p. 312). But the spectator's involvement in the hero's imaginary world could entail not only "enjoyable identification with the passion represented," but also the "positivization of the negative," in which characters and social norms are portrayed as "pretentious, empty of substance and ridiculous" (pp. 312–13). In other words, the positivization of the negative, (that is, gaining an insight into the comic behavior of characters) could make cathartic identification lead to detachment rather than involvement in the action of the play.

5. *Ironic Identification.*

Ironic identification refers to the state in which the spectator is jolted out of his involvement by the destruction of illusions.[63] Ironic identification is "the norm-breaking function par excellence." In the aesthetic state that Jauss calls "ironic identification" the spectator is deliberately outwitted or disappointed.

Jauss's typology of identification is dominated by the concept of catharsis; in fact, all the categories of the typology can be subsumed under catharsis, because they do not seem to be as mutually exclusive as Jauss prefers to think of them. Catharsis could be both norm-fulfilling (in the sense that the spectator's experience could be both social and aesthetic) and norm-breaking (in the sense that the spectator could refuse the aesthetic experience presented in front of him). If we follow Jauss's argument, cathartic identification could be associative (the spectator is immersed in the action of the play), or admiring (because the spectator could admire the model presented), or sympathetic (because the hero is "imperfect," suffering from a tragic flaw he is unaware of), or ironic, since the spectator can refuse to identify with the action presented. Jauss himself has even expressed uncertainty about the exact location of the cathartic identification in his own scheme (p. 297, n. 25). Such objections in no way vitiate Jauss's insight into the various experiences that are subsumed under catharsis. In fact, Jauss has recently been concerned with the exploration of different strata of meanings and the concepts behind catharsis:

> In Jauss's recent writings, the two former aspects of literature, poiesis (production) and aisthesis (reception) are . . . complemented by the third, mediating category of catharsis (communication), which is meant to account for the norm-constructive functions of literature and the role of emotions in literary reception.[64]

Jauss's emphasis on catharsis as communication—besides his earlier insights in which catharsis has a social, moral, and aesthetic functions— would enrich our understanding of how literature is received, how it functions, and how it transforms its readers. Indeed, Jauss has affirmed that catharsis provides "the possibility of [creating] a new attitude" in the reader.[65]

As the epigraph at the beginning of this chapter suggests, catharsis in modern critical theory tends to be regarded in terms of communication. Jauss's major interest in catharsis lies in his investigation of it as a communicative framework within which social change is introduced. In this way catharsis becomes a tool of social change in the sphere of literary artifacts, in the sense that the audience either tries to emulate the model (the hero), or refuses to do so. In both instances, in both acceptance and refusal, catharsis is the means. The audience identifies or refuses to identify with the model, and his identification or detachment performs a social function. In the case of identification, the audience will have an example to follow; in the case of detachment, the audience will have a bad character that it will avoid or reject emulating.

Another generalization about catharsis in modern critical theory is the extent to which the term is stretched beyond its Aristotelian concept. Some critics consider catharsis in connection with the religious, the comic, the imaginary, and so forth. Others discuss catharsis not through identification but through detachment. Both methods of investigation will lead to the same result: in order to understand identification, we have to understand detachment, and the opposite is also true. These divergent interests and different aspects of catharsis are indicative not only of the vitality of the concept, but of its relevancy to modern critical thought, no matter by what name we call such interests.

CHAPTER 6 Conclusion

What we call the beginning is often the end
And to make an end is to make a beginning
The end is where we start from
—T. S. ELIOT

CATHARSIS IS as important and relevant to modern literary criticism as it has always been. Its meaning has changed from age to age and from critic to critic throughout the history of literary criticism. I have pointed out the major reorientations in its interpretations, such as the emergence of the author-catharsis in the Romantic period, and Richard McKeon's pioneering studies of Aristotle's system of thought and terminology. Each age gives a different meaning to catharsis, a meaning relevant to its intellectual concerns: in the Renaissance, because of various philosophical, theological, religious, and political factors, secular critics gave catharsis a moral interpretation. In the Augustan Age, identification emanating from verisimilitude was thought to lead to catharsis as purgation. In the Romantic age, the poet became the center of attention, and so writings about catharsis changed from considerations about the audience to those about the poet himself. In the nineteenth century, Jakob Bernays revived the therapeutic interpretation of catharsis, and his publication on catharsis enjoyed an unusual popularity among the educated class, not to mention literary critics. Freud, under the influence of Bernays, adopted the term "cathartic treatment" to refer to an early form of the psychoanalytic method of treatment. Because the cathartic treatment was associated with hypnosis, Freud discarded the term "catharsis" from his vocabulary, and he opted instead for "free association," although up to a certain point in Freud's life, the technique of free association was at least similar to the cathartic treatment.

Freud's use of catharsis marked the birth of modern psychoanalysis, and to an extent catharsis became the cornerstone of psychoanalysis. That Freud used catharsis and later discarded the term was of great consequence to literary criticism. Critics who are not sympathetic to psychoanalysis mistakenly associate catharsis with what they pejoratively call "psychologizing" literature. Ironically, the same critics who dismiss catharsis as not worth thinking about, talk about it by using different terms. This phenomenon is evidence of the importance of catharsis in identifying a salient concept about literature and its function. Another consequence of Freud's use of catharsis was the way catharsis was pursued and studied by other psychologists, especially the ego psychologists. Literary critics sympathetic to Freud's insights into literature have found the development of catharsis most fruitful in helping them to explain such problems as identification, emotions, and the way in which we consider emotions as conducive to cognition.

In the past forty years or so, catharsis has been the subject of two contending parties: the psychoanalytic critics who favor it and study it, and the Formalist critics who dismiss it and denigrate it. Characteristically, most Formalists end up using different terms but with similar connotations, while others face the problematic meaning of catharsis directly and discuss it seriously. The serious discussion of catharsis is, however, not restricted to critics who use psychoanalytic literary theory; a host of others who belong to different schools of literary criticism have addressed themselves to the full ramifications of catharsis, and, despite Formalistic reservations, have gone on debating and discussing its meaning. Such debates and discussions are testimony not only to the relevance of catharsis to modern criticism, but also to its inescapable pertinence to the purpose and function of all forms of imaginative literature, in the way people of all times and places have responded to it.

Although by no means a simple aesthetic response, catharsis can be reduced to two elements: 1) emotional arousal that leads to 2) intellectual understanding. This oversimplifies the complexity of the problem, but it is useful in that it signifies the beginning and the end of the cathartic process, the reaction and understanding that occur in a spectator or reader when catharsis has been experienced. These general observations then follow. Catharsis begins by the arousal of the audience's (addressee's, recipient's, reader's, spectator's) emotions. These emotions are contradictory, and when they are reconciled, they leave the audience with a sense of repose, or reconciliation. The repose or serenity of the audience and its members after watching a play comes from their understanding of the causes of the action and incidents of the play. This basic understanding is derived from ratiocination combined with the serenity caused by the reconciliation of contradictory emotions (itself a form of understanding). Understanding could be of different types: psychological, moral, metaphysical, or whatever.

I have concentrated on tragedy to show the interest in catharsis by all schools of critical thought, but catharsis is much more. No matter by what name you call it, an explanation of catharsis is an explanation of the aesthetic phenomenon that takes place when we read a book, see a tragedy, listen to a piece of music, or look at a painting. Each of these is an aesthetic experience, but the degree of the involvement of the recipient with the medium, among other factors, determines the extent of emotional involvement and catharsis. Catharsis, then, points to the function of art where the audience's emotions are excited, and such emotions lead to intellectual understanding; in other words, the cathartic experience presupposes the harmony, and not the dichotomy, of emotions and cognition. In fact, from the point of view of catharsis, cognition, in the wider sense of the word, is only possible after we recognize the role of emotions. Most Formalists, disputing this, stipulate the separation of emotions and cognition. They think that cognition and detached ideation are enough for a meaningful aesthetic response. Their separation of emotions and cognition is artificial and ultimately detrimental to our understanding of the function of art. The aesthetic response that is catharsis presupposes the unity and interrelatedness of the emotions with the intellect; understanding, which comes from the exercise of the intellect, therefore results from the exercise of emotions. It is a phenomenon that even the Formalists cannot deny. Their constant references to "moving the reader" or that "poetry leads to wisdom" is their way of bringing catharsis into their discussions.

Since art serves a cathartic function (that is, the interrelatedness of emotions and cognitions), catharsis, no matter by what name we call it, will be debated, not because it does or does not exist but because there is constant argument about which part of the cathartic process should take precedence. It is without question an issue central to the importance and study of the purpose, significance, and function of literature in individuals and in society.

BIBLIOGRAPHY OF
WORKS CITED

Abrams, M. H. *The Mirror and the Lamp: Romantic Theory and the Critical Tradition.* New York: Oxford University Press, 1953.

Adams, Hazard. *The Interests of Criticism: An Introduction to Literary Theory.* New York: Harcourt, Brace & World, 1969.

———, ed. *Critical Theory Since Plato.* New York: Harcourt, Brace, Jovanovich, 1971.

Arnold, Matthew. "The Study of Poetry (1880)." In *Modern Criticism: Theory and Practice,* edited by Walter Sutton and Richard Foster. New York: Odyssey Press, 1963.

Austin, Allen. *T. S. Eliot: The Literary and Social Criticism.* Bloomington: Indiana University Press, 1971.

Bathrick, David. "The Politics of Reception Theory in the GDR." *Minnesota Review* NS 5 (1975): 125–33.

Belsey, Catherine. *Critical Practice.* London: Methuen & Co., 1980.

Bennett, Tony. *Formalism and Marxism.* London: Methuen & Co., 1979.

Bentham, Jeremy. *Essay on Logic.* In *Works,* vol. 7, edited by John Bowering. Edinburgh: William Tait, 1837.

Blackmur, R. P. "A Critic's Job of Work." In *Literary Opinion in America,* edited by Morton Zabel, pp. 770–790. New York: Harper & Brothers, 1937.

———. *Eleven Essays in the European Novel.* New York: Harcourt, Brace & World, 1964.

———. *The Lion and the Honeycomb: Essays in Solicitude and Critique.* 1933. Reprint. N.Y.: Harcourt, Brace & World, 1955.

Bodkin, Maud. *Archetypal Patterns in Poetry.* New York: Oxford University Press, 1948.

Booth, Wayne. "Notes and Exchanges." *Critical Inquiry* 3 (1976): 407–23; 4 (1977): 204–205.

Bosanquet, Bernard. *History of Aesthetic.* London: George Allen & Unwin, 1892.

Bradbury, John M. *The Fugitives: A Critical Account.* New Haven, Conn.: College & University Press, 1958.

Brandell, Gunnar. *Freud: A Man of His Century.* Translated by Ian White. Sussex: Harvester Press, 1974.

Breuer, Joseph and Sigmund Freud. *Studies in Hysteria.* Translated by A. A. Brill. New York: Nervous and Mental Disease Publishing Co., 1936.

Brill, A. A. *The Basic Writings of Sigmund Freud.* 1936. Reprint. New York: Modern Library, 1966.

———. *Freud's Contribution to Psychiatry.* 1944. Reprint. New York: Norton Publishing Co., 1962.

———. *Fundamental Conceptions of Psychoanalysis.* New York: Harcourt, Brace & Co., 1921.

Brooks, Cleanth. "I. A. Richards and *Practical Criticism.*" *Sewanee Review* 89 (1981): 586–95.

———. *Modern Poetry and the Tradition.* New York: Oxford University Press, 1965.

———. "The State of Criticism: A Sampling." *Sewanee Review* 65 (1957): 484–98.

———. *The Well Wrought Urn: Studies in the Structure of Poetry.* 1947. Reprint. New York: Harcourt, Brace & World, 1975.

Brown, J. A. C. *Freud and the Post-Freudians.* Baltimore: Penguin Books, 1961.

Brunius, Teddy. "Catharsis." *Dictionary of the History of Ideas.* Edited by Philip P. Wiener. New York: Charles Scribner's Sons, 1968.
————. *Inspiration and Katharsis.* Uppsala: Uppsala University 1966.
Burke, Kenneth. "Catharsis—Second View." *Centennial Review of Arts and Sciences,* 5 (1961): 107–32.
————. "The Criticism of Criticism." *Accent,* 15 (1955): 279–92.
————. "On Catharsis or Resolution." *Kenyon Review* 21 (1959): 337–75.
Butcher, S. H. *Aristotle's Theory of Poetry and Fine Art.* 1894. Reprint. New York: Dover Publication, 1951.
Bywater, Ingram. *Aristotle on the Art of Poetry.* London: Oxford University Press, 1909.
————. "Milton and the Aristotelian Definitions of Tragedy." *Journal of Philology* 27 (1901): 267–75.
Cassirer, Ernst. *An Essay on Man.* New Haven, Conn.: Yale University Press, 1944.
Coakly, Jay J. *Sport in Society: Issues and Controversies.* 2d ed. St. Louis: C. V. Mosby Co., 1982.
Cratty, Bryant J. *Psychology in Contemporary Sports: Guidelines for Coaches and Athletes.* 2d ed. Englewood Cliffs: Prentice-Hall, 1983.
Crews, Frederick C. "Literature and Psychology." In *Relations of Literary Study: Essays on Interdisciplinary Contributions.* Edited by James Thorpe, pp. 73–87. New York: Modern Language Association, 1967.
Culler, Jonathan. "Prolegomena to a Theory of Reading." In *The Reader in the Text: Essays on Audience and Interpretation,* edited by Susan Suleiman and Inge Crossman. Princeton, N.J.: Princeton University Press, 1980.
————. *Structuralist Poetics: Structuralism, Linguistics, and the Study of Literarure.* Ithaca, N.Y.: Cornell University Press, 1975.
Dahiyat, Ismail M. *Avicenna's Commentary on the Poetics of Aristotle.* Leiden: E. J. Brill, 1974.
Daiches, David. *Critical Approaches to Literature.* London: Longman Press, 1956.
Dalma, Juan. "La catarsis en Aristoteles, Bernays y Freud." *Revista de Psiquiatria y Psicologia Medical* 6 (1963): 257–69.
Detweiler, Robert. *Story, Sign and Self: Phenomenology and Structuralism as Literary-Critical Methods.* Philadelphia: Fortress Press, 1978.
Dodds, E. R. *The Greeks and the Irrational.* Berkeley and Los Angeles: University of California Press, 1951.
Edel, Leon. "Literature and Biography." In *Relations of Literary Study: Essays on Interdisciplinary Contributions,* edited by James Thorpe, pp. 57–72. New York: Modern Language Association, 1967.
Eidelberg, Ludwig. *Encyclopedia of Psychoanalysis.* New York: Free Press, 1968.
Eliot, T. S. *The Sacred Wood.* London: Faber and Faber, 1922.
————. *Selected Essays.* Rev. ed. New York: Harcourt, Brace & World, 1960.
————. *The Use of Poetry and the Use Criticism.* London: Faber and Faber, 1938.
Eliot, Valerie. *The Waste Land: A Facsimile and Transcript of the Original Draft Including the Annotations of Ezra Pound.* New York: Harcourt, Brace, Jovanovich, 1971.
Ellenberger, Henri F. *The Discovery of the Unconscious: The History and Evolution of Dynamic Psychiatry.* New York: Basic Books, 1970.
Else, Gerald F. *Aristotle's Poetics.* Ann Arbor: University of Michigan Press, 1967.
————. *Aristotle's Poetics: The Argument.* Cambridge: Harvard University Press, 1957.

———. "Survey of Work on Aristotle's *Poetics,* 1940–1954." *Classical Weekly* 48 (1954–55): 73–82.

Erlich, Victor. *Russian Formalism: History, Doctrine.* Rev. ed. The Hague: Mouton Co., 1965.

———. "Russian Formalism." *Journal of the History of Ideas* 34 (1973): 27–38.

———. "Russian Formalism." *The Princeton Encyclopedia of Poetry and Poetics,* edited by Alex Preminger, Frank J. Warnke, and O. B. Hardison, Jr. Princeton, N.J.: Princeton University Press, 1974.

Fekete, John. *The Critical Twilight: Explorations in the Ideology of Anglo-American Literary Theory from Eliot to McLuhan.* London: Routledge & Kegan Paul, 1977.

Fenichel, Otto. *The Psychoanalytic Theory of Neurosis.* New York: Norton Publications, 1945.

Ferenczi, Sandor. *Contributions to Psychoanalysis.* Translated by Ernest Jones. Toronto: Copp Clark, 1916.

———. *Further Contributions to the Theory and Technique of Psycho-Analysis.* 1926. Reprint. London: Hogarth Press, 1950.

———. "The Principle of Relaxation and Neo-Catharsis." *International Journal of Psychoanalysis* 11 (1930): 428–43.

Fokkema, D. W. and Elrud Kunne-Ibsch. *Theories of Literature in the Twentieth Century: Structuralism, Marxism, Aesthetics of Reception, Semiotics.* London: C. Hurst & Co., 1977.

Foster, Richard. *The New Romantics: A Reappraisal of the New Criticism.* Bloomington: Indiana University Press, 1962.

Fraiberg, Louis. *Psychoanalysis and American Literary Criticism.* Detroit: Wayne State University Press, 1960.

Frank, Armin Paul. *Kenneth Burke.* New York: Twayne Publishers, 1969.

Frank, Jerome D. and Florence B. Powderwater. "Group Psychotherapy." In *American Handbook of Psychiatry.* vol. 2, edited by Silvano Arieti, pp. 1362–74. New York: Basic Books, 1959.

Frye, Northrop. *Anatomy of Criticism: Four Essays.* Princeton, N.J.: Princeton University Press, 1957.

———. *T. S. Eliot: An Introduction.* Chicago: University of Chicago Press, 1963.

Gibb, J. R. "The Effects of Human Relations Training." In *Handbook of Psychotherapy and Behavior Change: An Empirical Analysis,* edited by Allen E. Bergin and Sol L. Garfield, pp. 839–62. New York: Wiley & Sons, 1971.

Gilbert, Allan H., ed. *Literary Criticism: Plato to Dryden.* New York: American Book Co., 1940.

Golden, Leon. "Catharsis." *Transactions and Proceedings of the American Philological Association* 113 (1962): 51–60.

———. "Mimesis and Catharsis." *Classical Philology* 64 (1969): 145–53.

———, and O. B. Hardison, Jr. *Aristotle's Poetics: A Translation and Commentary for Students of Literature.* Englewood Cliffs: Prentice Hall, 1968.

Goldstein, Harvey D. "Mimesis and Catharsis Reexamined." *Journal of Aesthetics and Art Criticism* 24 (1966): 567–77.

Gould, Thomas. "Review of Else's, *Aristotle's Poetics: The Argument.*" *Gnomon* 34 (1962): 641–49.

Graff, Gerald. *Literature Against Itself: Literary Ideas in Modern Society.* Chicago: Chicago University Press, 1979.

———. *Poetic Statement and Critical Dogma.* Evanston, Ill.: Northwestern University Press, 1970.

Gras, Vernon W., trans. and ed. *European Literary Theory and Practice: From*

Existential Phenomenology to Structuralism. New York: Dell Publishing Co., 1973.

Greenson, R. R. *The Technique and Practice of Psychoanalysis.* New York: International Universities Press, 1967.

Hankiss, Elmer. "A Comparative Study of Tragic Catharsis." In *Proceedings of the International Comparative Literature Association: 2: Comparative Literature Today: Theory and Practice*, edited by Eva Kushner and Roman Struc, pp. 565–71. Stuttgart: Bieber, 1979.

Hathaway, Baxter. *The Age of Criticism: The Late Renaissance in Italy.* Ithaca, N.Y.: Cornell University Press, 1962.

———. "Catharsis." *Dictionary of World Literature.* edited by Joseph Shipley. Totowa, N.J.: Littlefield, Adams, 1972.

———. "John Dryden and The Function of Tragedy." *PMLA* 58 (1943): 664.

Hawkes, Terence. *Structuralism and Semiotics.* Berkeley and Los Angeles: University of California Press, 1977.

Heller, Ágnes. "Lukács's Aesthetics." *The New Hungarian Quarterly* 7 (1966): 84–94.

Hinckley, Robert G. and Lydia Hermann. *Group Treatment in Psychotherapy: A Report of Experience.* Minneapolis: University of Minnesota Press, 1951.

Hohendahl, Peter Uwe. "Introduction to Reception Aesthetics." Trans. Marc Silberman. *New German Critique* 10 (1977): 29–63.

Holland, Norman N. "Criticism as Transaction." In *What is Criticism*, edited by Paul Hernadi. Bloomington: Indiana University Press, 1981.

———. *The Dynamics of Literary Response.* New York: Oxford University Press, 1968.

———. *5 Readers Reading.* New Haven: Yale University Press, 1975.

———. "Literary Interpretation and the Three Phases of Psychoanalysis." *Critical Inquiry* 3 (1976): 221–33.

———. *Poems in Persons: An Introduction to the Psychoanalysis of Literature.* New York: Norton Publications, 1973.

———. "A Transactive Account of Transactive Criticism." *Poetics* 7 (1978): 177–89.

———. "Unity Identity Text Self." *PMLA* 90 (1975): 813–22.

Holland, Virginia. *Counterpoint: Kenneth Burke and Aristotle's Theories of Rhetoric.* New York: Philosophical Library, 1959.

Hyman, Stanley Edgar. *The Armed Vision: A Study in the Methods of Modern Literary Criticism.* Rev. abr. ed. New York: Random House, 1955.

Iser, Wolfgang. *The Act of Reading: A Theory of Aesthetic Response.* Baltimore: Johns Hopkins University Press, 1978.

———. *The Implied Reader: Patterns of Communication in Prose Fiction from Bunyan to Beckett.* Baltimore: Johns Hopkins University Press, 1974.

Jauss, Hans Robert. *Aesthetic Experience and Literary Hermeneutics.* Translated by Michael Shaw. Minneapolis: University of Minnesota Press, 1982.

———. "Interview with Hans R. Jauss." Translated by Marilyn S. Fries. *Diacritics* 5 (1975): 53–61.

———. "Levels of Identification of Hero and Audience." *New Literary History* 5 (1974): 283–317.

———. "Literary History as a Challenge to Literary Theory." *New Literary History* 2 (1970): 7–37.

———. "Theses on the Transition from the Aesthetics of Literary Works to a Theory of Aesthetic Experience." In *Interpretation of Narrative*, edited by Mario J. Valdés and Owen J. Miller, pp. 137–47. Toronto: University of Toronto Press, 1978.

———. *Toward an Aesthetic of Reception.* Translated by Timothy Bahti. Minneapolis: University of Minnesota Press, 1982.

Jensen, H. James. *A Glossary of John Dryden's Critical Terms.* Minneapolis: University of Minnesota Press, 1969.

Jones, Ernest. *The Life and Work of Sigmund Freud.* Vol. 1. New York: Basic Books, 1953.

————. "Obituary." *International Journal of Psychoanalysis* 14 (1933): 463–66.

————. *What is Psychoanalysis?* New York: International Universities Press, 1948.

Joyce, James. *A Portrait of the Artist as a Young Man.* London: Heinemann, 1973.

Kaplan, Morton and Robert Kloss. *The Unspoken Motive: A Guide to Psychoanalytic Literary Criticism.* New York: Free Press, 1973.

Kauffmann, Walter. *From Shakespeare to Existentialism.* Boston: Beacon Press, 1959.

Kazin, Alfred. *On Native Grounds: An Interpretation of Modern American Literature.* New York: Anchor Press, 1956.

Kirkwood, G. M. "Review of Else's *Aristotle's Poetics:* The Argument." *The Classical Journal* 55 (1959): 36–39.

Kitto, H. D. F. "Catharsis." In *The Classical Tradition: Literary and Historical Studies in Honor of Harry Caplan,* edited by Luitpold Wallach, pp. 133–47. Ithaca, N.Y.: Cornell University Press, 1966.

Krieger, Murray. "Contextualism." *The Princeton Encyclopedia of Poetry and Poetics,* edited by Alex Preminger, Frank J. Warnke, and O. B. Hardison, Jr. Princeton, N.J.: Princeton University Press, 1974.

————. "Contextualism Was Ambitious." *Journal of Aesthetics and Art Criticism* 21 (1962): 81–88.

————. *The New Apologists for Poetry.* Minnesota: University of Minnesota Press, 1956.

————. *The Play and Place of Criticism.* Baltimore: Johns Hopkins University Press, 1967.

————. *Theory of Criticism: A Tradition and its System.* Baltimore: Johns Hopkins University Press, 1976.

————. *The Tragic Vision: Variations on a Theme in Literary Interpretation.* New York: Holt, Rinehart and Winston, 1960.

Kris, Ernst. *Psychoanalytic Explorations in Art.* New York: International Universities Press, 1952.

Kuhns, Richard. *The House, The City, and The Judge: The Growth of Moral Awareness in the Oresteia.* Indianapolis: Bobbs-Merrill, 1962.

Leland, Bradford P.; Jack R. Gibb; and Kenneth D. Benne, eds. *T-Group Therapy and Laboratory Method: Innovation in Re-education.* New York: John Wiley & Sons, 1964.

Lemon, Lee T. and Marrion J. Reis. *Russian Formalist Criticism: Four Essays.* Lincoln: University of Nebraska Press, 1965.

Lentricchia, Frank. *After the New Criticism.* Chicago: University of Chicago Press, 1980.

Lesser, Simon O. *Fiction and the Unconscious.* Boston: Beacon Press, 1957.

————. "Tragedy, Comedy, and the Esthetic Experience." *Literature and Psychology* 6 (1956): 131–39.

Lieberman, M. A.; I. A. Yalom; and M. B. Miles. *Encounter Groups: First Facts.* New York: Basic Books, 1973.

Lorand, Sandor. "Sandor Ferenczi." *Encyclopedia of Psychoanalysis,* edited by Ludwig Eidelberg. New York: Free Press, 1968.

Lovejoy, Arthur O. *Essays in the History of Ideas.* Baltimore: Johns Hopkins University Press, 1948.

Lukács, Georg. "Introduction to a Monograph on Aesthetics." In *Marxism and Art: Essays Classic and Contemporary,* edited by Maynard Solomon, pp. 404–19. Detroit, Mich.: Wayne State University Press, 1979.

McKeon, Richard. "Literary Criticism and the Concept of Imitation in Antiquity." In *Critics and Criticism: Ancient and Modern,* edited by R. S. Crane et al. Chicago: University of Chicago Press, 1952.

Mailloux, Steven. *Interpretive Conventions: The Reader in the Study of American Fiction.* Ithaca, N.Y.: Cornell University Press, 1982.

Mannoni, O. *Freud.* Translated by Renand Bruce. New York: Pantheon Books, 1971.

Marx, Karl. *Grundrisse: Foundations of the Critique of Political Economy.* Translated by Martin Nicholaus. Hammondsworth, England: Penguin Books, 1973.

Matthiessen, F. O. *The Achievement of T. S. Eliot.* 3d ed. New York: Oxford University Press, 1958.

Mizner, Arthur. "Recent Criticism." *Southern Review* 5 (1939): 376–400.

Moreno, J. L. *Mental Catharsis and the Psychodrama.* New York: Beacon Press, n.d.

————. *Sociodrama.* New York: Beacon House, 1944.

————. "Psychodrama." In *American Handbook of Psychiatry.* Vol. 2. Edited by Silvano Arieti, pp. 1375–96. New York: Basic Books, 1959.

Moreno, J. L. and James M. Enneis. *Hypnodrama and Psychodrama.* New York: Beacon House, 1950.

Morgan, George Allen, Jr. *What Nietzsche Means.* Cambridge: Harvard University Press, 1941.

Morris, Ruth. "The Novel as Catharsis." *Psychoanalytical Review* 31 (1944): 88–104.

Mueller, Gustav E. "The Hegel Legend of Thesis, Antithesis and Synthesis." *Journal of the History of Ideas* 19 (1958): 411–14.

Natenberg, Maurice. *The Case-history of Sigmund Freud: A Psycho-Biography.* Chicago: Regent House, 1955.

Nelson, Benjamin, ed. *Sigmund Freud on Creativity and the Unconscious.* New York: Harper and Row, 1958.

Neubaur, John. "Trends in Literary Reception: Die neuer Leiden der Wertherwirkung." *German Quarterly* 52 (1979): 69–79.

Nichols, Michael R. and Melvin Zax. *Catharsis in Psychotherapy.* New York: Gardner Press, 1977.

Nietzsche, Friedrich. *The Birth of Tragedy and the Case of Wagner.* Translated and introduced by Walter Kaufmann. New York: Random House, 1967.

Oberndorf, Clarence P. "Psychoanalysis in Literature and its Therapeutic Value." *Psychoanalysis and the Social Sciences* 1 (1947): 297–310.

Ogden, C. K.; I. A. Richards; and James Wood. *The Foundations of Aesthetics.* London: George Allen & Unwin, 1922.

Paolucci, Anne and Henry, eds. *Hegel on Tragedy.* New York: Doubleday, 1962.

Pottle, Frederick A. "Catharsis." *Yale Review* 40 (1951): 621–41.

Rabinowitz, Peter. "Truth in Fiction: A Reexamination of Audiences." *Critical Inquiry* 4 (1977): 121–41.

Ransom, John Crowe. *The New Criticism.* Norfolk, Conn.: New Direction, 1941.

————. "The Understanding of Fiction." *Kenyon Review* 12 (1950): 189–218.

————. *The World's Body.* New York: Charles Scribner's Sons, 1938.

Richards, I. A. *Principles of Literary Criticism.* New York: Harcourt, Brace, and Jovanovich, 1925.

————. *Complementaries: Uncollected Essays.* Edited by John Paul Russo. Manchester, England: Carcanet New Press, 1976.

Rieff, Philip. *Freud: The Mind of the Moralist.* New York: Viking Press, 1959.

Riviere, Joan, trans. and ed. *Collected Papers of Sigmund Freud.* Vol. 1. New York: International Psychoanalytic Press, 1924.

Rosenmeyer, T. G. "Review of G. Else's *Aristotle's Poetics: The Argument.*" *American Journal of Philology* 80 (1959): 310–14.

Rueckert, William H. *Kenneth Burke and the Drama of Human Relations.* Minneapolis: University of Minnesota Press, 1963.

————, ed. *Critical Responses to Kenneth Burke, 1924–1966.* Minneapolis: University of Minnesota Press, 1969.

Sahakian, William and Mabel L. Sahakian. *Ideas of the Great Philosophers.* New York: Barnes & Noble, 1966.

Sanborn, H. "A Sidelight on Katharsis." *Classical Journal* 33 (1937–38): 322–35.

Scaliger, J. C. "Poetics." In *Critical Theory Since Plato*, edited by Hazard Adams, pp. 137–43. New York: Harcourt, Brace, Jovanovich, 1971.

Scheff, T. J. *Catharsis in Healing, Ritual, and Drama.* Berkeley and Los Angeles: University of California Press, 1979.

Schneider, Daniel E. *The Psychoanalyst and the Artist.* 1950. Reprint. New York: New American Library, 1979.

Scholes, Robert. *Structuralism in Literature: An Introduction.* New Haven: Yale University Press, 1974.

Segers, Rien T. "Readers, Text and Author: Some Implications of Rezeptionsästhetik." *Yearbook of Comparative and General Literature* 24 (1975): 15–23.

Shelley, P. Bysshe. *Defence of Poetry.* Edited by Albert S. Cook. Boston: Ginn & Co., 1890.

Slavson, S. R. "Catharsis in Group Psychotherapy." *Psychoanalytic Review* 38 (1951): 39–52.

Spector, Jack. *The Aesthetics of Freud: A Study in Psychoanalysis and Art.* New York: Praeger Press, 1972.

Spingarn, Joel. *A History of Literary Criticism in the Renaissance.* 2d ed. New York: Columbia University Press, 1908.

Stanford, W. B. "On a Recent Interpretation of the Tragic Catharsis." *Hermathena* 85 (1955): 52–56.

Strachey, James, ed. *The Standard Edition of the Complete Psychological Works of Sigmund Freud.* 24 vols. London: Hogarth Press, 1953–74.

Strupp, Hans H. *An Introduction to Freud and Modern Psychoanalysis.* New York: Barron's Educational Services, 1967.

Suleiman, Susan R. and Inge Crosman, eds. *The Reader in the Text: Essays on Audience and Interpretation.* Princeton, N.J.: Princeton University Press, 1980.

Sutton, Walter. "The Contextualist Dilemma–or Fallacy." *Journal of Aesthetics and Art Criticism* 17 (1958): 219–29.

————. "Contextualist Theory and Criticism as a Social Act." *Journal of Aesthetics and Art Criticism* 19 (1961): 317–25.

————. "Letters Pro and Con." *Journal of Aesthetics and Art Criticism* 21 (1963): 347.

———— and Richard Foster, eds. *Modern Criticism: Theory and Practice.* New York: Odyssey Press, 1963.

Tate, Allen. "The Aesthetic Emotion as Useful." *This Quarterly* 5 (1932): 292–303.

————. *Essays of Four Decades.* Chicago: Swallow Press, 1968.

Tate, J. "Tragedy and the Black Bile." *Hermathena* 50 (1937): 1–25.

Thompson, E. M. *Russian Formalism and Anglo-American New Criticism.* The Hague: Mouton Co., 1971.

Tompkins, Jane P., ed. *Reader-Response Criticism: From Formalism to Post-Structuralism.* Baltimore: The Johns Hopkins University Press, 1980.

Trilling, Lionel. *Freud and the Crisis of Our Culture.* Boston: Beacon Press, 1955.

――――. *The Liberal Imagination: Essays on Literature and Society.* New York: Viking Press, 1951.

Vivas, Eliseo. *The Artistic Transaction and Essays on Theory of Literature.* Columbus: Ohio University Press, 1963.

――――. "Contextualism Reconsidered." *Journal of Aesthetics and Art Criticism* 18 (1959): 222–40.

――――. *Creation and Discovery: Essays in Criticism and Aesthetics.* New York: Noonday Press, 1955.

Wellek, René. "Cleanth Brooks, Critic of Critics." *Southern Review* 10 (1974): 125–52.

――――. "The Criticism of T. S. Eliot." *Sewanee Review* 64 (1956): 398–443.

――――. *Four Critics: Croce, Valéry, Lukács and Ingarden.* Seattle: University of Washington Press, 1981.

――――. "The Literary Theory of William K. Wimsatt." *Yale Review* 66 (1976–77): 178–92.

――――. "The New Criticism: Pro and Contra." *Critical Inquiry* 4 (1977–78): 611–24.

――――. "Notes and Exchanges." *Critical Inquiry* 4 (1977): 203–206.

――――. "On Rereading Richards." *Southern Review* 3 (1967): 533–54.

―――― and Austin Warren. *Theory of Literature.* 1942. Reprint. New York: Harcourt, Brace & World, 1956.

Whalley, George. *Poetic Process: An Essay in Poetics.* Cleveland, Ohio: World Publishing Co., 1967.

Wheelwright, Philip. *The Burning Fountain: A Study in the Language of Symbolism.* Bloomington: Indiana University Press, 1954.

――――. "Mimesis and Katharsis: An Archetypal Consideration." In *English Institute Essays,* 1951. edited by Alan S. Downer, pp. 3–30. New York: Columbia University Press, 1952.

White, Hayden and Margaret Brose, eds. *Representing Kenneth Burke: Selected Papers from the English Institute, New Series, No. 6.* Baltimore: The Johns Hopkins University Press, 1982.

Wimsatt, W. K. *Day of the Leopards: Essays in Defense of Poems.* New Haven: Yale University Press, 1976.

――――. *Hateful Contraries: Studies in Literature and Criticism.* Lexington: University of Kentucky Press, 1965.

――――. *The Verbal Icon: Studies in the Meaning of Poetry.* Lexington, Ky.: University of Kentucky Press, 1954.

―――― and Monroe C. Beardsley. "The Affective Fallacy." *Sewanee Review* 57 (1949): 31–55.

―――― and Cleanth Brooks. *Literary Criticism: A Short History.* New York: Random House, 1957.

Winters, Yvor. *In Defense of Reason.* New York: Swallow Press, 1947.

――――. *The Function of Criticism: Problems and Exercise.* Denver, Colo.: Alan Swallow, 1957.

Wolman, Benjamin B. *The Unconscious Mind: The Meaning of Freudian Psychology.* Englewood Cliffs: Prentice-Hall, 1968.

Young, Robert. *Untying the Text: A Post-Structuralist Reader.* London: Routledge & Kegan Paul, 1981.

NOTES

Introduction

1. More recently, however, there have been attempts to minimize the importance of catharsis in literary criticism. M. D. Petrusevski, a Yugoslavian scholar, in a study published in *Ziva Antika*, vol. 2 (Skoplje, 1954), has even argued that Aristotle never used the word "catharsis" in his definition of tragedy in the *Poetics*. I had taken the importance of catharsis in Aristotle's *Poetics* for granted, and Petrusevski's objection was formidable. If I were to study catharsis seriously, I had to overcome the contention that catharsis in Aristotle's *Poetics* is "a red herring." The roots of modern contention about the importance of catharsis lie in Richard McKeon's pioneering study of the concept of "imitation," in his article, "Literary Criticism and the Concept of Imitation in Antiquity," *Modern Philology* (August 1936), reprinted in R. S. Crane et al., *Critics and Criticism: Ancient and Modern* (Chicago: University of Chicago Press, 1952), pp. 147–75. Although McKeon's article deals with Plato's and Aristotle's usage of "imitation," McKeon reaches the conclusion that one cannot, or should not, refer to different works of Aristotle to interpret a particular term, because of Aristotle's systematic division of knowledge into domains, each with its own terms and methodologies. Scholars have generally tried to interpret Aristotle's catharsis in the *Poetics* by referring to Aristotle's *Politics*. According to McKeon, such a practice is essentially faulty.

2.. I have deliberately avoided discussing catharsis in other fields. In anthropology, the emphasis on catharsis is the claim that tragedy plays an important role, as a scapegoat, in helping spectators rid themselves of psychic tensions or fears. In behavioral psychology, the emphasis is on catharsis as an agent that helps to overcome maladjustment. The Prague Structuralists think of catharsis as helping man get rid of his "automatic machine-like" routine and to move to a free and creative state. For these and other considerations see Elmer Hankiss, "A Comparative Study of Tragic Catharsis," in *Proceedings of the International Comparative Literature Association: 2: Comparative Literature Today: Theory and Practice*, eds. Eva Kushner and Roman Struc (Stuttgart: Bieber, 1979), p. 565.

3. These are clearly laid out and discussed in O. B. Hardison's "commentary," in Leon Golden and O. B. Hardison, Jr., *Aristotle's Poetics: A Translation and Commentary for Students of Literature* (Englewood Cliffs: Prentice-Hall, 1968), especially pp. 133–37.

4. "Art" will be used throughout this study as a synonym of imaginative literature in general: "reader" will be used synonymously with spectator, addressee, or recipient.

5. I have found the following references helpful in understanding the Hegelian Dialectic: Gustav E. Mueller, "The Hegel Legend of Thesis, Antithesis and Synthesis," *Journal of the History of Ideas* 19 (1958): 411–14; Bernard Bosanquet, *History of Aesthetic* (London: George Allen & Unwin, 1892), chaps. 2, 12; William S. Sahakian and Mabel L. Sahakian, *Ideas of the Great Philosophers* (New York: Barnes & Noble, 1966), pp. 140–41; and Anne and Henry Paolucci, eds. *Hegel on Tragedy* (New York: Doubleday, 1962), pp. 49–52.

6. Nietzsche's major ideas are discussed by Walter Kaufmann, trans., *The Birth of Tragedy and the Case of Wagner* (New York: Random House, 1967), introduction, pp. 3–13; George Allen Morgan, Jr., *What Nietzsche Means* (Cambridge: Harvard University Press, 1941); and Walter Kaufmann, *From Shakespeare to Existentialism* (Boston: Beacon Press, 1959).

7. Ernst Cassirer, *An Essay on Man* (New Haven, Conn.: Yale University Press, 1944), p. 148. Further references to this edition will appear in parentheses in the text.

8. The etymological origins of "protagonist" indicate two ideas: "first," and "contention."

9. A good description of Lukács's aesthetics is provided by the following: John Fekete, *The Critical Twilight: Explorations in the Ideology of Anglo-American Literary Theory from Eliot to McLuhan* (London: Routledge & Kegan Paul, 1977), pp. 224–25; Ágnes Heller, "Lukács's Aesthetics," *New Hungarian Quarterly* 7 (Winter, 1966): 84–94; and Lukács's "Introduction to a Monograph on Aesthetics," in *Marxism and Art: Essays Classic and Contemporary*, ed. Maynard Solomon (Detroit: Wayne State University Press 1979), pp. 404–19.

10. Ágnes Heller, "Lukács's Aesthetics," p. 88.

11. This means that we cannot experience catharsis from real life situations; a hint of why this occurs is explained in the *Poetics* when Aristotle says that we do not enjoy pain in reality, whereas the same pain is a source of pleasure in a tragedy. This conclusion leads me to label the use of catharsis in accounting for the aggression of spectators in sports as an "abuse" of the term. For such abuses of catharsis in sports, see Bryant J. Cratty, *Psychology in Contemporary Sports: Guidelines for Coaches and Athletes*, 2d ed. (Englewood Cliffs: Prentice Hall, 1983), pp. 94–95; and Jay J. Coakly, *Sport in Society: Issues and Controversies*, 2d ed. (St. Louis: C. V. Mosby Co., 1982), pp. 56–81.

12. This premise necessitates the audience's "suspension of disbelief" to experience catharsis. If a spectator were literally to attack the villain of a tragedy, out of ignorance of the conventions of theater, that spectator would not be experiencing catharsis.

13. One of the consequences of this premise is that what causes catharsis in a particular culture does not necessarily cause the same effect in an audience in a different culture. Moreover, if a play is directed toward a particular audience in a particular time, then the same play does not necessarily cause the same effect on an audience that lives in a different age. Kenneth Burke points out, for instance, that Jean Anouilh's *Antigone* (1944), when shown in Paris, reminded the French of the German occupation of Paris and had, because of the relationship of its subject matter to the occupation, a definite cathartic effect on the audience. When the same play was shown in the United States several years later, the play did not have a cathartic effect on the audience. There was no identification and little emotional arousal. The play was originally aimed at an audience that had lived through and understood the subject matter. The American audience simply was not "tuned in" to the allusions of the French situation. See Burke, "On Catharsis, or Resolution," *Kenyon Review* 21 (Summer, 1959): 362.

14. If we borrow the vocabulary of psychodrama (a topic that will be dealt with in detail in chapter 2), we can refine the general definition to distinguish several kinds of catharsis, some of which are self-evident. An individual's response in the cathartic process is called "individual catharsis." Collective response (that particular aspect of our response that we share with the others) is called "group catharsis." If we refer to the emotional arousal and excitation, then we have "somatic catharsis." Similarly, if we refer to the intellectual aspect of the cathartic process, there is "mental catharsis." Another important distinction is between the audience's catharsis ("primary catharsis") and the writer's catharsis ("secondary catharsis"), although in psychodrama "primary catharsis" refers to the actor's catharsis, and the "secondary catharsis" to the audience's.

15. A highly original approach that tries to find a common denominator that all definitions of catharsis share is offered by Elmer Hankiss. Hankiss postulates

that catharsis causes a change in the spectator's mind, which he thinks is a change of values from a lower level to a higher one. My only objection to this thesis is that since he thinks catharsis is a process that moves from a lower to a higher level, he makes the intellectual part superior to the emotional. Catharsis as I understand it values both emotional arousal and intellectual understanding equally. Neither is superior to the other. Neither occurs separately, and one leads to the other. Any change of focus or value on one or another part of this sequence creates a situation where the aesthetic experience should be described by a term other than catharsis. Catharsis is the result of both emotional arousal and cognitive understanding. They cannot be separated. See Hankiss, "A Comparative Study of Tragic Catharsis," pp. 565–71.

1. The Historical Meanings of Catharsis

1. Leon Golden and O. B. Hardison, Jr., *Aristotle's Poetics: A Translation and Commentary for Students of Literature* (Englewood Cliffs, N.J.: Prentice Hall, 1968), p. 11. I have chosen this translation deliberately, because, among other things, it highlights the point of argument through the awkward translation of the catharsis phrase.

2. Baxter Hathaway, "Catharsis," *Dictionary of World Literature*, ed. Joseph T. Shipley (Totowa, N.J.: Littlefield, Adams, 1972).

3. Actually Aristotle's *Poetics*, through the Arabic version, exerted its influence much earlier than this date. The first known Arabic version of Aristotle's treatise was made by Abu-Baschar about 935. Two centuries later, Averroes made an abridgment in Arabic that was eventually translated into Latin in the thirteenth century by Hermann. The number of Arabic versions of Aristotle's *Poetics* is still a matter of dispute; see Ismail M. Dahiyat's introduction to *Avicenna's Commentary on the Poetics of Aristotle* (Leiden: E. J. Brill, 1974), especially pp. 3–12.

4. Gerald F. Else, *Aristotle's Poetics: The Argument* (Cambridge: Harvard University Press, 1957), pp. 443–44.

5. Other useful classifications can be found in Richard Kuhns, *The House, the City, and the Judge: The Growth of Moral Awareness in the Oresteia* (Indianapolis: Bobbs-Merrill, 1962), pp. 105–16; Else, *The Argument*, p. 225; Teddy Brunius, "Catharsis," *Dictionary of the History of Ideas*, ed. Philip P. Wiener (New York: Charles Scribner's Sons, 1968); Teddy Brunius, *Inspiration and Katharsis* (Uppsala: Uppsala University, 1966), pp. 60–67; Leon Golden and Hardison, *Aristotle's Poetics*, pp. 133–37; Ingram Bywater, *Aristotle on the Art of Poetry* (London: Oxford University Press, 1909), pp. 159–60. Almost all the classifications, except Hardison's, are based on what catharsis means for a particular critic or commentator. Hardison's classifications are based on the way the catharsis phrase has been translated. My approach takes the *Poetics* as a point of departure. Rather than relying on what catharsis has come to mean, I take the text of the *Poetics* as a polarity around which different critics and commentators have congregated.

6. Leon Golden, "Catharsis," *Transactions and Proceedings of the American Philological Association* 113 (1962): 55. For a different view, which emphasizes the commonness of the word, see H. D. F. Kitto, "Catharsis," in *The Classical Tradition: Literary and Historical Studies in Honor of Harry Caplan*, ed. Luitpold Wallach (Ithaca, N.Y.: Cornell University Press, 1966), pp. 135, 140.

7. J. Tate, "Tragedy and the Black Bile," *Hermathena* 50 (1937): 3.

8. Frederick A. Pottle, "Catharsis," *Yale Review* 40 (June, 1951): 621–22.

9. For a detailed discussion of these two usages, see Tate, "Tragedy and the Black Bile," p. 4; Pottle, "Catharsis," p. 622; W. B. Stanford, "On a Recent

Interpretation of the Tragic Catharsis," *Hermathena,* 85 (1955): 52–53; and Kuhns, *The House, the City, and the Judge,* pp. 106–108.

10. Kitto, "Catharsis," p. 135.

11. E. R. Dodds, *The Greeks and the Irrational* (Berkeley and Los Angeles: University of California Press, 1951). According to Dodds, both Plato and Theophrastus, for example, believed that music was beneficial for the treatment of anxiety (p. 80).

12. Ibid., p. 65.

13. Tate, "Tragedy and the Black Bile," p. 4.

14. Pottle, "Catharsis," p. 622.

15. Milton actually echoes the ideas of different Italian Renaissance critics. See the excerpt of Minturno's *L'Art Poetica,* in Joel Spingarn, A History of Literary Criticism in the Renaissance, 2d ed. (New York: Columbia University Press, 1908), p. 80: "As a physician eradicates, by means of poisonous medicine, the perfervid poison of disease which affects the body, so tragedy purges the mind of its perturbations by the force of these emotions beautifully expressed in verse." Another detailed study of the Italian Renaissance critics and their different translations of catharsis is also offered by Ingram Bywater in "Milton and the Aristotelian Definitions of Tragedy," *Journal of Philology* 27 (1901): 267–75. Bywater offers (p. 272) an interesting discussion of the Italian critic Scaino and his understanding of catharsis in medical terms. It is interesting to note that Scaino understood and rendered catharsis in rhetorical terms: "purgatio," "expiatio," and "lustratio." It is beyond the scope of this study to try to trace the relationship between rhetoric and catharsis. For a more concise and varied treatment of the Renaissance views, see the article "Catharsis" by Hathaway in *Dictionary of World Literature.*

16. For a more detailed study of Bernays, see Franz Susemihl and R. D. Hicks, *The Politics of Aristotle* (London: Macmillan and Co., 1894), especially "Note on *Katharsis,*" pp. 641–56; S. H. Butcher, *Aristotle's Theory of Poetry and Fine Art,* 4th ed. (Reprint: New York: Dover Publications, 1951), p. 244ff; and Else, *The Argument,* pp. 225, 440–42.

17. Bywater, *Aristotle on the Art of Poetry,* p. 17.

18. Ibid., p. 17.

19. Spingarn, *A History of Literary Criticism in the Renaissance,* p. 3.

20. Giraldi Cinthio in *Literary Criticism: Plato to Dryden,* ed. Allan H. Gilbert (New York: American Book Co., 1940), p. 252.

21. Spingarn actually rejects the ethical consideration (p. 76), and prefers to call it "aesthetic." I take Spingarn's "aesthetic" to mean something like "appealing to our sense of beauty, and devoid of any practical sides or considerations." If this is so, then Robertello's criticism was against the moral trend of his age. But since Robertello regards tragedy an instrument of "hardening the emotions" of the spectators, and since his views of the role of tragedy are purely functional, I cannot see how it could be called aesthetic, unless we are willing to admit that the aims of group psychology (and this is what I understand Robertello to be alluding to) could be understood in terms of aesthetic values.

22. Julius Caesar Scaliger, "Poetics," in *Critical Theory Since Plato,* ed. Hazard Adams (New York: Harcourt, Brace, Jovanovich, 1971), p. 142.

23. Baxter Hathaway, "John Dryden and the Function of Tragedy," *PMLA* 58 (1943): 665.

24. A detailed exposition of the views of the major critics of the time is offered by B. Hathaway, ibid., pp. 665–67.

25. H. James Jensen, *A Glossary of John Dryden's Critical Terms* (Minneapolis: University of Minnesota Press, 1969) p. 29.

26. Quoted by M. H. Abrams, *The Mirror and the Lamp: Romantic Theory and the Critical Tradition* (New York: Oxford University Press, 1953), p. 139.

27. *Defence of Poetry*, ed. Albert S. Cook (Boston: Ginn & Co., 1890), p. 35.

28. For a detailed study of the romantics' use of catharsis, see Abrams, *The Mirror and the Lamp*, pp. 138–48.

29. Reprinted in R. S. Crane et al., *Critics and Criticism: Ancient and Modern* (Chicago: University of Chicago Press, 1952), pp. 147–75.

30. Richard McKeon, "Literary Criticism and the Concept of Imitation in Antiquity," in *Critics and Criticism: Ancient and Modern*, ed. R. S. Crane et al. (Chicago: University of Chicago Press, 1952), p. 160.

31. Ibid., p. 161.

32. Ibid., p. 166.

33. Else, *Aristotle's Poetics: The Argument*, p. 439. In addition, see pp. 225–32, 437–43 for his evaluation and rejection of the different theories advanced to explain catharsis. Else also studies the difficulties that arise when catharsis is explained by relying on external evidence.

34. Ibid., p. 439.

35. Else, *Aristotle's Poetics* (Ann Arbor: University of Michigan Press, 1967), p. 25.

36. Among the critics who challenge Else's interpretation, see Harvey D. Goldstein, "Mimesis and Catharsis Reexamined," *Journal of Aesthetics and Art Criticism* 24 (Summer, 1966): 577, n. 18; Brunius misreads and misconstrues Else, and thus his objection to Else's interpretation is based on the passage in the *Politics* (which Else repeatedly warns against using), see Brunius, *Inspiration and Katharsis*, p. 57. Among Else's reviewers, see, for instance, Thomas G. Rosenmeyer, *American Journal of Philology* 80 (January, 1950): 314; G. M. Kirkwood, *Classical Journal* 55 (October, 1959): 38; and Thomas Gould, *Gnomon* 34 (December 1962): 642.

37. Golden, "Catharsis," pp. 51–60; Golden, "Mimesis and Catharsis," *Classical Philology*, 64 (1969): 145–53; Golden and Hardison, Jr., *Aristotle's Poetics*, pp. 116–18, and p. 133.

38. Golden, "Catharsis." pp. 52, 58, 59.

39. Kitto, "Catharsis," p. 138.

40. Ibid., pp. 142–143. Kitto's emphasis.

41. Ibid., p. 143.

42. Ibid., p. 144.

43. Quoted by Else, "Survey of Work on Aristotle's *Poetics*, 1940–1954," *Classical Weekly* 48 (1954–55):78.

44. Herbert Sanborn, "A Sidelight on Katharsis," *Classical Journal* 33 (1937–38): 324.

45. Stanford, "On a Recent Interpretation of the Tragic Catharsis," p. 52.

46. Philip Wheelwright, *The Burning Fountain: A Study in the Language of Symbolism* (Bloomington: Indiana University Press, 1954), quoted by Kuhns, *The House, the City, and the Judge*, pp. 113–15.

47. This interpretation, which emphasizes the redemptive process, is obviously religious. Wheelwright acknowledges the "minor importance" religion had for Aristotle, but Wheelwright treats the *Poetics* not as "an end in itself, but mainly as an instrument for the clearer and fuller understanding of Greek tragic drama." See his article, "Mimesis and Katharsis: An Archetypal Consideration," in *English Institute Essays, 1951*, ed. Alan S. Downer (New York: Columbia University Press, 1952), p. 22.

48. Kuhns, *The House, the City, and the Judge*, p. 113.

49. An interesting discussion of the "aesthetic triad" is offered by George Whalley in his *Poetic Process: An Essay in Poetics* (Cleveland, Ohio: World Publishing Co., 1967), p. 11.

50. In James Joyce's *A Portrait of the Artist as a Young Man* (1916), chapter

5, the dialogue between Stephen Daedalus and Lynch provides a similar aesthetic theory. Joyce uses Aristotle's terminology, but defines "pity" as "the feeling which arrests the mind in the prescence of whatsoever is grave and constant in human sufferings and unites it with the human sufferer." Joyce also defines "fear" or "terror" as "the feeling which arrests the mind in the presence of whatsoever is grave and constant in human sufferings and unites it with the secret cause" (p. 189, Heineman ed.). Joyce, however, makes an important distinction between two emotions: the tragic emotion or the aesthetic one is static because "the mind is arrested and raised" and the kinetic emotion (of desire or loathing) is generated by "improper arts" because "desire urges us to possess, to go to something, while loathing urges us to abandon, to go from something." The arts that excite them, pornographic or didactic, are therefore improper arts (p. 190). Joyce's distinction between the "static emotion" and the "kinetic emotion" is reminiscent of the stages of mystical revelation where complete inaction leads to transcendence, whereas the "kinetic emotion"—the one that leads to action for or against is thought to be detrimental to mystical revelation. That happens because the essence of mysticism is to exercise discipline over rational thinking, which urges one to "possess," "take," or "go after."

I am indebted to Professor Barnstone for pointing out the similarity between the effect of tragic catharsis and the notion of change from stasis to ekstasis in mysticism.

2. Catharsis in Psychoanalysis

1. Henri F. Ellenberger, *The Discovery of the Unconscious: The History and Evolution of Dynamic Psychiatry* (New York: Basic Books, 1970), p. 484.

2. Ibid., p. 561, n. 280. Jakob Bernays says that between the first edition of his treatise on catharsis (1857) and the second (1878), "no less than 70 works were published in Germany on the topic." Moreover, after the second edition, 80 more works were published on the topic. See Juan Dalma, "La catarsis en Aristoteles, Bernays y Freud," *Revista de Psiquiatria Y Psicologia Medical* 6 (1963): 257.

3. O. Mannoni, *Freud*, trans. Renard Bruce (New York: Pantheon Books, 1971), p. 25; and Maurice Natenberg, *The Case-History of Sigmund Freud: A Psycho-Biography* (Chicago: Regent House, 1955), p. 109.

4. Ellenberger, *The Discovery of the Unconscious*, p. 484, and Sandor Ferenczi, "The Principle of Relaxation and Neo-Catharsis," *International Journal of Psychoanalysis* 11 (1930): 429.

5. Ernest Jones, *The Life and Work of Sigmund Freud*, (New York: Basic Books, 1953), 1: 225n, 244n.

6. There is evidence, however, that Freud might have met Jakob Bernays. See Freud's letter to Martha Bernays on the 23 July 1881, and Jones, *Life and Work of Freud*, 1: 100.

7. James Strachey, ed. *The Standard Edition of the Complete Psychological Works of Sigmund Freud* (London: Hogarth Press, 1953), 1: 40 [hereafter *Standard Edition* S.E.]. I have not restricted myself to the *Standard Edition* because of the many objections leveled against its accuracy. I have used A. A. Brill's translations, whenever possible, because he was the first to introduce Freud's ideas and books to English, and also because the particular terminology he used for "catharsis" and "abreaction," which later were accepted by other translators, are relevant to the discussion of catharsis in psychology.

8. Joseph Breuer and Sigmund Freud, *Studies in Hysteria*, trans. A. A. Brill (New York: Nervous and Mental Disease Publishing Co., 1936), pp. 20, 21, 15, and 27. Further references to this edition will appear in parenthesis in the text.

9. Benjamin B. Wolman, *The Unconscious Mind: The Meaning of Freudian Psychology* (Englewood Cliffs: Prentice-Hall, 1968), p. 162.

10. Natenberg, *The Case-History of Sigmund Freud,* p. 109.

11. Breuer and Freud, *Studies,* pp. 77–78.

12. "Freud's psychology" is generally referred to as "psychoanalysis." Psychologists who left the psychoanalytic movement opted for a different term. Thus, Jung refers to his psychology as "analytic," and A. Adler refers to his as "individual psychology." See J. A. C. Brown, *Freud and the Post-Freudians* (Hammondsworth: Penguin Books, 1961), p. 1.

13. Wolman, *The Unconscious Mind,* p. 162.

14. Hans H. Strupp, *An Introduction to Freud and Modern Psychoanalysis* (New York: Barron's Educational Services, 1967), p. 90; Ludwig Eidelberg, *Encyclopedia of Psychoanalysis* (New York: Free Press, 1968); and Sandor Ferenczi, *Contributions to Psychoanalysis,* trans. Ernest Jones (Toronto: Copp Clark, 1916), p. 25.

15. Jack Spector, *The Aesthetics of Freud: A Study in Psychoanalysis and Art* (New York: Praeger Press, 1972), p. 102.

16. Dalma, "La catarsis," p. 253.

17. *SE,* 1: xxxi.

18. Ibid., 19:191.

19. Ibid., 22: 5–182.

20. Benjamin Nelson, ed. *Sigmund Freud on Creativity and the Unconscious* (New York: Harper and Row, 1958), p. 45. Emphasis added. Also in *SE,* 9: 141.

21. *SE,* 18:7.

22. Ibid., p. 17.

23. Joan Riviere, ed., *Collected Papers of Sigmund Freud* (New York: International Psychoanalytic Press, 1924), 1:265.

24. Besides *Studies,* Freud discussed the cathartic treatment and its problems several times. See especially the following: "The Psychotherapy of Hysteria," *SE,* 2: 255–305; "Freud's Psychoanalytic Procedure," *SE,* 7: 249–54; "On Psychotherapy," *SE,* 7: 257–68; "On the History of the Psycho-analytic Movement," *SE,* 14: 7–66; "A Short Account of Psychoanalysis," *SE,* 19: 191–209; and "An Autobiographical Study," *SE,* 20: 7–70. For easy access, all references are made to the *Standard Edition.*

25. R. R. Greenson, *The Technique and Practice of Psychoanalysis* (New York: International Universities Press, 1967), 1: 13.

26. Otto Fenichel, *The Psychoanalytic Theory of Neurosis* (New York: Norton, 1945), p. 562.

27. The paper was first published in the *Psychoanalytic Quarterly* 11 (1942): 459–64, and appears in SE, 7: 305–10. Further references to this paper will be to Strachey's translation in the *SE,* and they will appear in the text. Incidentally, Freud never mentions catharsis in the article by name, not even once, probably because of its association with the cathartic treatment and hypnosis.

28. Freud's acceptance of Bernays's interpretation of catharsis as the purging of emotions and Freud's interest in catharsis have led to speculations linking Aristotle to Bernays and finally to Freud. Juan Dalma in his paper, "La catarsis," pp. 253–69, has speculated about the relationship between Bernays and Freud and the subsequent "cathartic treatment."

29. See also Freud's discussion of the suffering rebel hero in "Totem and Taboo" (1912), in *The Basic Writings of Sigmund Freud,* trans. A. A. Brill (1936; reprint ed., New York: Modern Library, 1966), pp. 926–27.

30. I am drawing on Philip Rieff's excellent discussion of catharsis and the

function of art in Freud. See Rieff's *Freud: The Mind of the Moralist* (New York: Viking Press, 1959), pp. 345–53.

31. *SE*, 18: 17. Emphasis added. Rieff quotes this passage to justify his claim that it expresses Freud's earlier views on art. Despite his perceptive observations and insights, Rieff seems to me to be off the mark here. Freud says explicitly that first it is "abreaction" and then "self-mastery" that the children achieve in their play. Why Rieff failed to see the line of thought in the very passage he quotes is unclear to me.

32. *SE*, 21: 210; "Goethe Address," ibid., 208–12.

33. Rieff, *Freud*, p. 349.

34. Sandor Lorand, "Sandor Ferenczi," in *Encyclopedia of Psychoanalysis*, ed. Ludwig Eidelberg, (New York: Free Press, 1968), pp. 140–46.

35. Ernest Jones, "Obituary," *International Journal of Psychoanalysis* 14 (1933): 463.

36. For a brief discussion of these methods, see J. A. C. Brown, *Freud and the Post-Freudians* (Baltimore: Penguin Book, 1961), p. 51.

37. Sandor Ferenczi, *Further Contributions to the Theory and Technique of Psycho-Analysis* (1926; reprint ed., London: Hogarth Press, 1950), p. 199.

38. Brown, *Freud*, p. 52.

39. A. A. Brill, *Fundamental Conceptions of Psychoanalysis* (New York: Harcourt, Brace and Co., 1921), p. 310.

40. A. A. Brill, *Freud's Contribution to Psychiatry* (1944, reprint ed., New York: Norton, 1962), p. 174. Further references to this edition will appear in parentheses in the text.

41. This, of course, is true when we extend Ferenczi's psychoanalytic findings to literature.

42. I have used the following useful introductory studies for writing this section: Jerome D. Frank and Florence B. Powderwater, "Group Psychotherapy," in *American Handbook of Psychiatry*, ed. Silvano Arieti (New York: Basic Books, 1959), 2: 1362–74; and J. L. Moreno, "Psychodrama," ibid., 1375–96; M. A. Lieberman, I. D. Yalom, and M. B. Miles, *Encounter Groups: First Facts* (New York: Basic Books, 1973); and Michael R. Nicholas and Melvin Zax, *Catharsis in Psychotherapy* (New York: Gardner Press, 1977), chap. 5, pp. 65–87.

43. Robert G. Hinckley and Lydia Hermann, *Group Treatment in Psychotherapy: A Report of Experience* (Minneapolis: University of Minnesota Press, 1951), p. 17.

44. Nichols and Zax, *Catharsis in Psychotherapy*, p. 66.

45. S. R. Slavson, "Catharsis in Group Psychotherapy," *Psychoanalytic Review* 38 (1951): 41.

46. Ibid.

47. The technique employed in psychodrama varies: sometimes the patient acts as an actor without audience; at other times there is an audience. People taking part in the psychodrama on the stage are called "auxiliary egos," and they assist the patient in various ways, such as performing and imitating his actions on the stage. If psychodrama is used for group therapy, it is called *sociodrama;* if hypnosis is used, it is called *hypnodrama.* See J. L. Moreno , *Sociodrama* (New York: Beacon House, 1944; and J. L. Moreno and James M. Enneis, *Hypnodrama and Psychodrama* (New York: Beacon House, 1950).

48. J. L. Moreno, *Mental Catharsis and the Psychodrama* (New York: Beacon House, n.d.), p. 209. Further references to the book will appear in parentheses in the text.

49. Moreno, *Sociodrama*, p. 2. The rift between fantasy and reality in Moreno's scheme seems to correspond to T. S. Eliot's conception of the rift

between emotion and intellect.

50. Rieff, *Freud*, p. 348n.

51. Moreno and Enneis, *Hypnodrama and Psychodrama*, p. 10. Moreno's emphasis.

52. K. D. Benne, "History of the T-Group in the Laboratory Setting," in *T-Group Theory and Laboratory Method: Innovation in Re-education*, ed. Leland P. Bradford, Jack R. Gibb, and Kenneth D. Benne (New York: John Wiley & Sons, 1964), p. 81. Further references to this article will appear in parentheses in the text.

53. Nichols and Zax, *Catharsis in Psychotherapy*, p. 80. Further references to this edition will appear in parentheses in the text.

54. J. R. Gibb, "The Effects of Human Relations Training," in A. E. Bergin and S. L. Garfield, eds., *Handbook of Psychotherapy and Behavior Change* (New York: Wiley, 1971), p. 78.

55. Berkeley: University of California Press.

3. Psychological Criticism and Catharsis

1. That Freud was concerned only with the psychology of the artist and the responses of the audience is an oversimplification. Freud shows three basic trends in his writings on art: an interest in the work of art alone, similar to the Formalist Critics (as in "The Moses of Michelangelo" [1914]); an interest in the psychology of the artist (as in "Creative Writers and Day-Dreaming" [1908]); and a study of responses and identification in the audience ("Psychopathic Characters on the Stage" [1905 or 1906, but published in 1942]). I have restricted my study to the second and third trends, since Freud's Formalist thinking is not germane to the discussion of catharsis.

2. Ernest Jones, *What is Psychoanalysis?* (New York: International Universities Press, 1948), p. 92.

3. See, Leon Edel, "Literature and Biography," in *Relations of Literary Study: Essays on Interdisciplinary Contributions*, ed. James Thorpe (New York: Modern Language Association, 1967), pp. 69–70. See also Frederick C. Crews's excellent article "Literature and Psychology," ibid., especially pp. 80–81.

4. Ruth Morris, "The Novel as Catharsis," *Psychoanalytical Review* 31 (1944): 104. Further references to this article will appear in parentheses in the text.

5. Clarence P. Oberndorf, "Psychoanalysis in Literature and its Therapeutic Value," *Psychoanalysis and the Social Sciences* 1 (1947): 301.

6. Louis Fraiberg, *Psychoanalysis and American Literary Criticism* (Detroit: Wayne State University Press, 1960), p. 224.

7. Lionel Trilling, *Freud and the Crisis of Our Culture* (Boston: Beacon Press, 1955), p. 34.

8. Both articles are reprinted in Trilling's *The Liberal Imagination: Essays on Literature and Society* (New York: Viking Press, 1951), pp. 34–57, 160–80.

9. Trilling, *The Liberal Imagination*, p. 54. Further references to this edition will appear in parentheses in the text.

10. See Baxter Hathaway's excellent discussion of the mithridatic interpretation of catharsis and the way he links Trilling to Renaissance critics in his *The Age of Criticism: The late Renaissance in Italy* (Ithaca, N.Y.: Cornell University Press, 1962), p. 207, n. 2, and pp. 226–29.

11. Surprisingly enough, Louis Fraiberg praises Trilling's interpretation of catharsis as homeopathy and hails it as "a fine example of the creative use of psychoanalytic concepts in criticism which extends our understanding in appro-

priate directions through both psychological and literary experience" (p. 214 of *Psychoanalysis and American Literary Criticism*). Homeopathy is not a "fine example of the use" of psychology in criticism, neither is it "creative." The concept of homeopathy has been associated with catharsis for hundreds of years, and it is only Fraiberg's inadequate knowledge of the history of literary criticism that makes him praise the one aspect of Trilling's thought that is the least original.

12. Ernst Kris, *Psychoanalytic Explorations in Art* (New York: International Universities Press, 1952). Further references to this edition will appear in parentheses in the text.

13. Morton Kaplan and Robert Kloss, *The Unspoken Motive: A Guide to Psychoanalytic Literary Criticism* (New York: Free Press, 1973), p. 224.

14. Ibid., p. 222.

15. Another psychoanalytic investigation of identification is offered by Daniel E. Schneider in "One Psychoanalytic View of the Arts," in his *The Psychoanalyst and the Artist* (1950; reprint ed., New York: New American Library, 1979), pp. 226–33. Schneider emphasizes catharsis as a sequential process.

16. The centrality of catharsis to Burke's critical thought is echoed by one of his most sympathetic readers in the following lengthy passage:

> All of Burke's thinking about literature as poetic, grammatical, rhetorical, and ethical-personal verbal action culminates in the theories of tragedy and catharsis. . . . The essence of tragedy, Burke says, is the cathartic function which it performs, the purging of the audience's bodily, personal, civic, and religious irresolutions. By this route, Burke goes from poetry to drama to tragedy to catharsis (the term around which the dramatistic theory of literature is built) and back to poetry. Catharsis is also one of the key terms around which his whole system is built, for though it belongs to the poetry-drama-tragedy cluster, it also belongs to the order-cluster. . . . This means that in any discussion of catharsis Burke will logologically "radiate out" and consider the negative victimage, mortification, hierarchy, redemption, and categorical guilt. By this logic, all are implicit in the term "catharsis" and, by implication, in the terms "poetry," "drama," and "tragedy," since catharsis links the two clusters.

William H. Rueckert, *Kenneth Burke and the Drama of Human Relations* (Minneapolis: University of Minnesota Press, 1963), p. 208.

17. Kenneth Burke, "On Catharsis, or Resolution," *Kenyon Review* 21 (1959): 337–75 (reference to this article will appear in the text as OCOR); and "Catharsis—Second View," *Centennial Review of Arts and Sciences*, 5 (1961): 107–32 (reference to this article will appear in the text as CSV).

18. William Rueckert, *Kenneth Burke*; Virginia Holland, *Counterpoint: Kenneth Burke and Aristotle's Theories of Rhetoric* (New York: Philosophical Library, 1959); Armin Paul Frank, *Kenneth Burke* (New York: Twayne Publishers, 1969); William Rueckert, ed., *Critical Responses to Kenneth Burke, 1924–1966* (Minneapolis: University of Minnesota Press, 1969); and Hayden White and Margaret Brose, eds., *Representing Kenneth Burke: Selected Papers From the English Institute, New Series, No. 6* (Baltimore: The Johns Hopkins University Press, 1982).

19. Kenneth Burke, "The Criticism of Criticism," *Accent* 15 (1955): 292. Burke's emphasis.

20. Simon O. Lesser, *Fiction and the Unconscious* (Boston: Beacon Press, 1957). Further references to this edition appear in parentheses in the text. Some other important books applying psychoanalytical insights to literature are Kris, *Psychoanalytic Explorations of Art* (1952); Schneider, *The Psychoanalyst and the Artist*, (which were both written by professional psychoanalysts and deal with the general field of aesthetics rather than with just fiction); and Maud Bodkin, *Archetypal Patterns in Poetry* (1948), which applies Carl G. Jung's ideas to her analysis of poetry and pays only lip service to Freud's ideas of psychoanalysis.

21. Kaplan and Kloss, *The Unspoken Motive*, p. 227.
22. In Hazard Adams, ed., *Critical Theory Since Plato* (New York: Harcourt, Brace, Jovanovich, 1971), p. 335.
23. Simon Lesser, "Tragedy, Comedy, and the Esthetic Experience," *Literature and Psychology* 6 (1956): 131–39. Reprinted as chapter 11 in *Fiction and the Unconscious*, pp. 269–93.

4. Catharsis in Formalist Criticism

1. Both articles are reprinted in W. K. Wimsatt, *The Verbal Icon: Studies in the Meaning of Poetry* (Lexington: University of Kentucky Press, 1954), pp. 3–18, 21–39.
2. Ibid., p. 282, n. 3.
3. The definitive study of Russian Formalism is Victor Erlich's *Russian Formalism: History, Doctrine*, rev. ed. (The Hague: Mouton Co., 1965); see also his article "Russian Formalism," *Journal of the History of Ideas* 34: (1973): 27–38.
4. See, for instance, the final chapter of Erlich's *Russian Formalism;* E. M. Thompson, *Russian Formalism and Anglo-American New Criticism* (The Hague: Mouton Co., 1971); Tony Bennett, *Formalism and Marxism* (London: Methuen & Co., 1979), p. 178, n. 3; see also the last paragraph of V. Erlich's excellent article "Russian Formalism" in *The Princeton Encyclopedia of Poetry and Poetics;* and Lee T. Lemon and Marrion J. Reis, *Russian Formalist Criticism: Four Essays* (Lincoln: University of Nebraska Press, 1965), pp. ix–xi.
5. Lemon and Reis, *Russian Formalist Criticism*, p. x.
6. Among the books that deal with this specific field of literary theory, see David Daiches, *Critical Approaches to Literature* (London: Longman Press, 1956), especially part 1, entitled "The Philosophical Inquiry," pp. 3–168: see also Murray Krieger, *Theory of Criticism: A Tradition and its System* (Baltimore: Johns Hopkins University Press, 1976), especially chap. 6, "Fiction, History, and Empirical Reality"; and Murray Krieger, *The New Apologists for Poetry* (Minneapolis: University of Minnesota Press, 1956), section 3, "The Function of Poetry: Science, Poetry, and Cognition."
7. Daiches, *Critical Approaches*, p. 50.
8. Ibid., p. 111.
9. Quoted by William K. Wimsatt and Cleanth Brooks, *Literary Criticism: A Short History* (New York: Random House, 1957), p. 449.
10. Matthew Arnold, "The Study of Poetry (1880)," in *Modern Criticism: Theory and Practice*, ed. Walter Sutton and Richard Foster (New York: Odyssey Press, 1963), p. 94.
11. See, for example, John Fekete, *The Critical Twilight: Explorations in the Ideology of Anglo-American Literary Theory from Eliot to McLuhan* (London: Routledge & Kegan Paul, 1977), p. 44; Gerald Graff, *Literature Against Itself: Literary Ideas in Modern Society* (Chicago: Chicago University Press, 1979), p. 147; and Catherine Belsey, *Critical Practice* (London: Methuen & Co., 1980), p. 15.
12. I. A. Richards, *Principles of Literary Criticism* (New York: Harcourt, Brace, and Jovanovich, 1925), pp. 47–48.
13. Ibid., p. 110.
14. Ibid., p. 113. Emphasis added.
15. René Wellek confirms my conclusions, "Richards's theory is thus a restatement of the affective theory of art which can be traced back to Aristotle's catharsis," "On Rereading Richards," *Southern Review* 3 (1967): 535.

16. C. K. Ogden, I. A. Richards, and James Wood, *The Foundations of Aesthetics* (London: George Allen & Unwin, 1922), p. 76.

17. Ibid., p. 84.

18. Richards, *Principles of Literary Criticism*, pp. 245–46. Richards's emphasis.

19. Ibid., p. 246. Emphasis added.

20. I. A. Richards, *Complementaries: Uncollected Essays*, ed. John Paul Russo (Manchester: Carcanet New Press, 1976), p. 9. The article from which the quotation is taken, "Emotion and Art," was first published in 1919.

21. Stanley Edgar Hyman, *The Armed Vision: A Study in the Methods of Modern Literary Criticism*, rev. abr. ed. (New York: Random House, 1955), p. 287.

22. See, for instance, Arthur Mizner, "Recent Criticism," *Southern Review* 5 (1939): 394; and René Wellek, "The Criticism of T. S. Eliot," *Sewanee Review* 64 (1956): 410.

23. T. S. Eliot, *Selected Essays*, rev. ed. (New York: Harcourt, Brace & World, 1960), pp. 6–7. Further references to this edition will appear in parentheses in the text.

24. Northrop Frye, *T. S. Eliot: An Introduction* (Chicago: University of Chicago Press, 1963), p. 29.

25. Wellek, "The Criticism of T. S. Eliot," p. 419. As far as I could ascertain, the first critic to make the observation that Eliot's critical thought reflects the cathartic principle is Hyman in his *The Armed Vision*, p. 65. Wellek follows Hyman by making the same observation in his article "The Criticism of T. S. Eliot," p. 408 and p. 409.

26. Eliot, *Selected Essays*, pp. 7–8.

27. Hyman, *The Armed Vision*, p. 66.

28. Valerie Eliot, *The Waste Land: A Facsimile and Transcript of the Original Draft including the Annotations of Ezra Pound* (New York: Harcourt, Brace, Jovanovich, 1971), p. 1.

29. Quoted by Wellek in "The Criticism of T. S. Eliot," p. 408.

30. Eliot, *Selected Essays*, p. 117.

31. Ibid., p. 125.

32. R. P. Blackmur, "A Critic's Job of Work," in *Literary Opinion in America*, ed. Morton Zabel (New York: Harper & Brothers, 1937), p. 784.

33. T. S. Eliot, Preface, *The Use of Poetry and the Use of Criticism* (London: Faber & Faber, 1938), p. 11.

34. Eliot, ibid., p. 138.

35. Ibid., p. 147.

36. Eliot, *Selected Essays*, p. 190.

37. F. O. Matthiessen, *The Achievement of T. S. Eliot*, 3d ed. (New York: Oxford University Press, 1958), p. 56.

38. T. S. Eliot, *The Sacred Wood* (London: Faber and Faber, 1922), p. x.

39. René Wellek, "The New Criticism: Pro and Contra," *Critical Inquiry* 4 (1977–80): 612.

40. Gerald Graff, *Literature Against Itself: Literary Ideas in Modern Society* (Chicago: University of Chicago Press, 1979), p. 141.

41. John Crowe Ransom, *The World's Body* (New York: Charles Scribner's Sons, 1938), p. 124.

42. Cleanth Brooks, *Modern Poetry and the Tradition* (New York: Oxford University Press, 1965), p. 147.

43. Allen Tate, "The Aesthetic Emotion as Useful," *This Quarterly* 5 (1932): 292.

44. Allen Tate, *Essays of Four Decades* (Chicago: Swallow Press, 1968), p. 202.

45. Quoted by Gerald Graff, *Literature Against Itself,* pp. 130, 131.

46. Ibid., p. 131. Graff's emphasis.

47. Richard Foster, *The New Romantics: A Reappraisal of the New Criticism* (Bloomington: Indiana University Press, 1962), pp. 135, 145. René Wellek has objected to the label several times. See, for example, his most recent objection and clarification of his critical position in his *Four Critics: Croce, Valéry, Lukács and Ingarden* (Seattle: University of Washington Press, 1981), pp. 56–57. Wayne Booth's "accusation" in *Critical Inquiry* 3:407–23 earned him a virulent reply in Wellek's letter in *Critical Inquiry* 4 (1977), see pp. 203–206.

48. John Crowe Ransom, *The New Criticism* (Norfolk, Conn.: New Direction, 1941), p. 201.

49. Ransom, *The World's Body,* p. 216.

50. Ransom, "The Understanding of Fiction," *Kenyon Review* 12 (1950): 202.

51. Foster, *The New Romantics,* p. 139.

52. Ransom, *The New Criticism,* p. 220.

53. Ibid., pp. 74–75.

54. Ransom, *The World's Body,* p. 193.

55. W. K. Wimsatt, *Hateful Contraries: Studies in Literature and Criticism* (Lexington: University of Kentucky Press, 1965), p. 76. Wimsatt's emphasis. A similar downgrading of the concept is declared by Wimsatt in *Literary Criticism: A Short History,* p. 37:

> [The interpretation of catharsis as lustration] has at least the advantage of making the enjoyment of tragedy occur while we are witnessing it, rather than in a sounder sleep when we get home, a relief after emotional orgy. Both views [i.e., of tragedy as purgation/purification and lustration] concern after all not what tragedy says or what tragedy is so much as what tragedy may do to us; they lie rather in the realm of experimental psychology than in that of literary criticism.

56. W. K. Wimsatt, *Day of the Leopards: Essays in Defense of Poems* (New Haven: Yale University Press, 1976), pp. 194–95.

57. W. K. Wimsatt, *The Verbal Icon: Studies in the Meaning of Poetry* (Lexington: The University of Kentucky Press, 1954), p. xvi.

58. René Wellek, "The Literary Theory of William K. Wimsatt," *Yale Review* 66 (1976–77): 191.

59. Yvor Winters, *In Defense of Reason* (New York: Swallow Press, 1947), pp. 552–53.

60. Yvor Winters, *The Function of Criticism: Problems and Exercises* (Denver, Colo.: Alan Swallow, 1957), pp. 160–61.

61. Yvor Winters, *In Defense of Reason,* p. 363.

62. Ibid., p. 363.

63. Ibid., p. 3.

64. Ibid., p. 29.

65. Yvor Winters, *The Function of Criticism,* pp. 103–104.

66. John M. Bradbury, *The Fugitives: A Critical Account* (New Haven, Conn.: College & University Press, 1958), p. 231; René Wellek, "Cleanth Brooks, Critic of Critics," *Southern Review* 10 (1974): 125.

67. Alfred Kazin, *On Native Grounds: An Interpretation of Modern American Literature* (New York: Anchor Books, 1956), pp. 311–49.

68. Gerald Graff, *Poetic Statement and Critical Dogma* (Evanston, Ill.: Northwestern University Press, 1970), p. 96. Compare, too, a similar statement by Graff in his *Literature Against Itself,* p. 142:

> Critics like Brooks might in one breath warn that poems are autonomous entities

with no claims to "truth of correspondence," only in the next to declare that poems yield profound truths about "the complexity of experience."

69. Cleanth Brooks, "The State of Criticism: A Sampling," *Sewanee Review* 65 (1957): 492–94.

70. Cleanth Brooks, "I. A. Richards and *Practical Criticism,*" *Sewanee Review* 89 (1981): 587.

71. Ibid., p. 589.

72. Wimsatt and Brooks, *Literary Criticism: A Short History,* p. 601.

73. Wellek, "Cleanth Brooks, Critic of Critics," p. 152.

74. Cleanth Brooks, *The Well Wrought Urn: Studies in the Structure of Poetry* (1947; reprint ed., New York: Harcourt, Brace & World, 1975), pp. 212–13. Brooks's emphasis.

Ransom, too, has referred to poetry as "intended to recover the dense and more refractory original world which we know loosely through our perceptions and memories." A similar universal notion of poetry and poets is held by R. P. Blackmur, who says in his Prefatory Note to *Eleven Essays in the European Novel* (New York: Harcourt, Brace & World, 1964), p. vii: "Speculation is endless, for me every good novel is a speculation—a theoretic form, a fresh psychology—a speculation in myth which reaches in to the driving psyche: the psyche which endures and even outlives human behavior." The novel (and we might as well use "poetry" in the general sense we have been using the term), gives us insights into universal values, the universal psyche. Besides, Blackmur has spoken of the task of criticism as the making of bridges between society and the arts, and that criticism is important because "the audience needs instruction in the skill of symbolic thinking." See *The Lion and the Honeycomb: Essays in Solicitude and Critique* (1933; reprint ed. New York: Harcourt, Brace & World, 1955), p. 206.

75. Quoted by Wellek, "The New Criticism: Pro and Contra," p. 617.

5. Catharsis in Recent Critical Theory

1. W. K. Wimsatt and Monroe C. Beardsley's "The Affective Fallacy" appeared in the *Sewanee Review* 57 (1949): 31–55; and was reprinted in W. K. Wimsatt, *The Verbal Icon: Studies in the Meaning of Poetry* (Lexington: University of Kentucky Press, 1954), pp. 21–39.

2. A good example of a structuralist who turned against structuralism is Roland Barthes's shift from structuralism to poststructuralism in his *S/Z* (1970). Robert Young discusses Barthes's shift from structuralism to poststructuralism in "Post Structuralism: An Introduction" in his *Untying the Text: A Post-Structuralist Reader* (London: Routledge & Kegan Paul, 1981), especially pp. 2–8.

3. A good discussion of European critical thought is offered by Vernon W. Gras in his introduction to *European Literary Theory and Practice: From Existential Phenomenology to Structuralism* (New York: Dell Publishing Co., 1973), pp. 1–23.

4. Jane P. Tompkins offers a brief survey of the changing role of the reader in criticism beginning with the classical period and ending with reader-response criticism in "The Reader in History: The Changing Shape of Literary Response," in her *Reader-Response Criticism: From Formalism to Post-Structuralism* (Baltimore: Johns Hopkins University Press, 1980), pp. 201–32. Despite serious omissions, such as Plato's discussion of the reader and also Aristotle's, the essay is a useful introduction to the concept of reader throughout the history of literary criticism.

5. Murray Krieger, "Contextualism," *The Princeton Encyclopedia of Poetry and Poetics,* p. 929.

6. I. A. Richards, *Principles of Literary Criticism* (New York: Harcourt, Brace, Jovanovich, 1925), p. 267. Richards's emphasis.

7. Cleanth Brooks, *The Well Wrought Urn* (1947; reprint ed., New York: Harcourt, Brace, & World, 1975), pp. 193–94.

8. Eliseo Vivas, *Creation and Discovery: Essays in Criticism and Aesthetics* (New York: Noonday Press, 1955), p. 107.

9. Murray Krieger, *The New Apologists for Poetry* (Minneapolis: University of Minnesota Press, 1956), p. 192.

10. Ibid., pp. 131–32.

11. Walter Sutton, "The Contextualist Dilemma—or Fallacy?" *Journal of Aesthetics and Art Criticism* [hereafter, JAAC] 17 (1958): 219–29; and "Contextualist Theory and Criticism as a Social Act," *JAAC* 19 (1961): 317–25. Vivas's reply to Sutton, "Contextualism Reconsidered," appeared in *JAAC* 18 (1959): 22–40, and was reprinted in Vivas, *The Artistic Transaction and Essays on Theory of Literature* (Columbus: Ohio State University Press, 1963), pp. 171–202. Murray Krieger, too, defends his teacher's ideas, and replies to Sutton in an article entitled "Contextualism Was Ambitious," in *JAAC* 21 (1962): 81–88, and the argument is closed by Sutton's "Letters Pro and Con," *JAAC* (1963): 347.

12. Hazard Adams, *The Interests of Criticism: An Introduction to Literary Theory* (New York: Harcourt, Brace & World, 1969), p. 119. Adams's statement seems to be a hasty generalization: Vivas's contextualism is an extension of not only the New Critical practice but its theory, too. We have already touched on some of the issues that Vivas develops from some of the New Critics, such as Richards's distinction between emotive language and the referential, and Brooks's contextual-referential dichotomy. Vivas, in fact, is something like the "spokesman" for the aesthetics of contextualism.

13. Ibid.

14. Compare in this respect Vivas's Neo-Platonic notion of art as bringing order to the chaotic world of everyday life in *Creation and Discovery*, p. xii: "The effects of art are carried into the mongrel world of actual men, the world of half-truth and half-dignity."

15. Vivas, *The Artistic Transaction*, p. 30.

16. Vivas, *Creation and Discovery*, p. 89.

17. Adams, *The Interests of Criticism*, p. 119.

18. Vivas, *Creation and Discovery*, p. 114.

19. Ibid., p. 188. Emphasis added.

20. Krieger, "Contextualism," p. 925.

21. Murray Krieger, *The Play and Place of Criticism* (Baltimore: Johns Hopkins University Press, 1967), pp. 226–27. Krieger also discusses tragedy and catharsis as "order" and "cosmic harmony" in his *The Tragic Vision: Variations on a Theme in Literary Interpretation* (New York: Holt, Rinehart and Winston, 1960), especially pp. 3–10.

22. Compare the statement made by Frank Lentricchia, *After the New Criticism* (Chicago: University of Chicago Press, 1980), p. 230:

Krieger inherits Vivas's traps and cannot help being caught in them. After the most strenuous efforts to bring poetry back to life from the deep freeze of aesthetic isolation he, like Vivas before him, becomes a victim of the very aestheticist and formalist error for which he has such well-warranted contempt.

23. Lentricchia offers the following insight, ibid., p. 235:

This complex vision [i.e., the poet making sublunary nature available to non-poets] is valorized as "mature" by T. S. Eliot, Brooks, Krieger, and the New Critics because it is a discovery of the true nature of things behind the veil of sleepy, quotidian living.

24. Jonathan Culler, *Structuralist Poetics: Structuralism, Linguistics, and the Study of Literature* (Ithaca, N.Y.: Cornell University Press, 1975), p. 257.

25. Robert Detweiler, *Story, Sign and Self: Phenomenology and Structuralism as Literary-Critical Methods* (Philadelphia: Fortress Press, 1978), p. 103.

26. Terence Hawkes, *Structuralism and Semiotics* (Berkeley and Los Angeles: University of California Press, 1977), p. 17.

27. Robert Scholes, *Structuralism in Literature: An Introduction* (New Haven, Conn.: Yale University Press, 1974), p. 207.

28. Northrop Frye, *Anatomy of Criticism: Four Essays* (Princeton, N.J.: Princeton University Press, 1957), p. 14. Further references to this edition will appear in parentheses in the text.

29. Frye says in two places in *The Anatomy of Criticism* that catharsis is Aristotle's central conception, on p. 66 and p. 210.

30. Frye also mentions catharsis in connection with comedy (p. 215); catharsis in terms of the poet (p. 301); and catharsis in biblical terms, by substituting pity and fear for "good and evil" (p. 326). I have not discussed his other considerations of catharsis because Frye gives us only passing, enigmatic remarks about them.

31. Tompkins, *Reader-Response Criticism*, p. x.

32. Peter Rabinowitz, "Truth in Fiction: A Reexamination of Audiences," *Critical Inquiry* 4 (1977): 121–41. Rabinowitz proposes four kinds of audiences: the actual audience, the authorial audience, the narrative audience, and the ideal narrative audience.

33. Tompkins, *Reader-Response Criticism*, p. ix.

34. Susan R. Suleiman and Inge Crosman, eds., *The Reader in the Text: Essays on Audience and Interpretation* (Princeton, N.J.: Princeton University Press, 1980), pp. 6–7.

35. Norman Holland, "Literary Interpretation and the Three Phases of Psychoanalysis," *Critical Inquiry* 3 (1976): 221–33.

36. Norman Holland, *The Dynamics of Literary Response* (New York: Oxford University Press, 1968). Further references to this edition will appear in parentheses in the text.

37. Norman Holland, "Unity Identity Text Self," *PMLA* 90 (1975): 813–22, reprinted in Tompkins, *Reader-Response Criticism*, pp. 118–33. Holland repeats twice in the same article the idea that we find in the literary work what we fear or wish most: in the passage above (p. 124) and on p. 125.

38. Holland, "Unity Identity," p. 125. See, also, Holland's concluding sentences in his essay "Criticism as Transaction" in *What Is Criticism?* edited by Paul Hernadi (Bloomington: Indiana University Press, 1981), p. 251.

39. Despite the various objections leveled against Holland's simplistic version of "identity theme" as a fixed mental construct, my concern is not to question Holland's model; rather, I am trying to explain catharsis within Holland's overall critical writings. For arguments against Holland's "identity theme," see Suleiman and Crosman, *The Reader in the Text*, p. 30, and Jonathan Culler's "Prolegomena to a Theory of Reading," in Suleiman and Crosman, *The Reader in the Text*, pp. 54–56.

40. Holland, *Dynamics*, p. 174.

41. Ibid., pp. 298–99.

42. Ibid., p. 75.

43. Wolfgang Iser, *The Implied Reader: Patterns of Communication in Prose Fiction from Bunyan to Beckett* (Baltimore: Johns Hopkins Univeristy Press, 1974). Further references to this edition will appear abbreviated as *(IR)* in parentheses in the text.

44. Iser is equivocal in his use of "strategy" and "repertoire." One example

taken from a single page will illustrate my point. In the *Act of Reading: A Theory of Aesthetic Response* (Baltimore: The Johns Hopkins University Press, 1978), p. 86, Iser says that "the repertoire of the text is made up of material selected from social systems and literary tradition." In the same paragraph, Iser affirms that "the strategies organize both the material of the text and the conditions under which that material is to be communicated." In the second paragraph of the same page Iser tells us that "the strategies of the text are replaced by personal organization." The problem is this: does the repertoire refer to the text or to the reader? And does strategy refer to the reader or the text? Apparently, Iser does not help us find the right answer, since "repertoire" for him consists of conventions, codes, and references (p. 93), but then if we try to explain this repertoire by using our own strategies as readers, we are confronted by Iser's enigmatic and confusing phrase, "the strategies of the text."

45. Iser, *The Act of Reading.* Further references to this edition will appear abbreviated as *(AOR)* in parentheses in the text.

46. It seems to me that Iser's reluctance to use catharsis might be attributed to professional and personal reasons. Both Iser and Jauss teach at the University of Constance in West Germany in the Department of Literature, which includes two other professors besides Iser and Jauss. Jauss is also a prominent critic, and catharsis is a central issue in his critical activity. It seems reasonable to conjecture as to the possibility of Iser distancing himself from Jauss. Such a distancing is hinted at when Iser declares that his "activity is concerned with [the] theory of response [which] has its roots in the text [whereas] a theory of reception [Jauss's] arises from a history of readers' judgments" (*Act of Reading*, p. x). I am thankful to Professor Rien T. Segers of the University of Groninegen (Netherlands) for providing me with the factual information concerning the University of Constance, but he is in no way responsible for my conjecture as to professional rivalry between Iser and Jauss; in fact, he opposes it.

47. Compare in this respect the Richardsian notion of balance in Iser's *Act of Reading*, p. 216. Other instances of Iser's moralizing attitudes occur in *Act of Reading*, pp. 157, 158, 230.

48. Peter Uwe Hohendahl, "Introduction to Reception Aesthetics," trans. Marc Silberman, *New German Critique* 10 (1977): 29.

49. For a good introduction to the diversity of reception aesthetics, see Rien T. Segers, "Readers, Text and Author: Some Implications of *Rezeptionsästhetik*," *Yearbook of Comparative and General Literature* 24 (1975): 15–23.

50. For a detailed study of reception in the GDR, see David Bathrick, "The Politics of Reception Theory in the GDR," *Minnesota Review*, NS 5 (1975): 125–33; Hohendahl, "Introduction to Reception Aesthetics," pp. 48–54; and John Neubaur, "Trends in Literary Reception: Die neuen Leiden Der Wertherwirkung," *German Quarterly* 52 (1979): 69–79.

51. Segers, "Readers, Text and Author," p. 15.

52. D. W. Fokkema and Elrud Kunne-Ibsch, *Theories of Literature in the Twentieth Century: Structuralism, Marxism, Aesthetics of Reception, Semiotics* (London: C. Hurst & Co., 1977), p. 138.

53. I am drawing on Hohendahl's excellent study "Introduction to Reception Aesthetics," p. 56.

54. Karl Marx, *Grundrisse: Foundations of the Critique of Political Economy*, trans. Martin Nicolaus (Hammondsworth, England: Penguin Books, 1973), p. 93. Compare Jauss's similar statement, "The productive and receptive aspects of the aesthetic experience are dialectically related," in "Thesis on the Transition from the Aesthetic of Literary Works to a Theory of Aesthetic Experience," in *Interpretation of Narrative* ed. Mario J. Valdé and Owen J. Miller (Toronto:

University of Toronto Press, 1978), p. 138. Further references to this article will appear in parentheses in the text.

55. Quoted by Fokkema and Kunne-Ibsch, *Theories of Literature,* p. 143.

56. Hans R. Jauss, "Literary History as a Challenge to Literary Theory," *New Literary History* 2 (1970): 7–37. Reprinted in a slightly different version in Hans R. Jauss, *Toward An Aesthetic of Reception,* trans. Timothy Bahti (Minneapolis: University of Minnesota Press, 1982), pp. 3–45.

57. Steven Mailloux, *Interpretive Conventions: The Reader in the Study of American Fiction* (Ithaca, N.Y.: Cornell University Press, 1982), pp. 166ff.

58. Hans R. Jauss, "Thesis on the Transition: from the Aesthetics of Literary Works to a Theory of Aesthetic Experience," in *Interpretation of Narrative,* ed. Mario J. Valdés and Owen J. Miller (Toronto: University of Toronto Press, 1978), p. 138.

59. Hans R. Jauss, "Levels of Identification of Hero and Audience," *New Literary History* 5 (1974): 284. Further references to this article will appear in parentheses in the text. A slightly different version of this article appears in Hans R. Jauss, *Aesthetic Experience and Literary Hermeneutics,* trans. Michael Shaw (Minneapolis: University of Minnesota Press, 1982), pp. 152–88.

60. In a somewhat similar statement in "Levels of Identification of Hero and Audience," Jauss hints at the role of mimesis in the cathartic process and regards mimesis (without mentioning the term) as intensifying our emotional involvement in a tragedy, p. 288:

> The imaginary object of tragedy, the separation between its action and the practical purposes of life, sets the spectator free in such a way that his emotion, his identification with the hero, can flare up more spontaneously, and consume itself more completely than in the context of everyday life.

61. Jauss, *Aesthetic Experience,* p. 92.

62. "Essay on Logic," in *Works,* ed. John Bowring (Edinburgh, 1837): 8: 272.

63. It seems to me that Jauss's terminology is inexact here: if the experience he calls "ironic identification" exclusively refers to the reader's detachment from an aesthetic experience, then why should we call it "identification?" A better term would be "ironic detachment," but Jauss apparently had to label such an aesthetic experience "ironic identification" since his typology takes identification as a criterion of studying reception.

64. Neubaur, "Trends in Literary Reception," p. 76.

65. "Interview with Hans R. Jauss," *Diacritics* 5 (1975), p. 57.

INDEX

Abreaction, 29–30, 33, 36, 38, 45, 49
Act of Reading, The (Iser), 106
Actors: in psychodrama, 40–41, 136n.47
Adams, Hazard, 94–95
Addressee. *See* Reader; Spectator
Admiring identification, 112, 113–14, 115
Aesthetic experience, 9, 83, 95–96, 102–103, 111–15, 119; Formalists on, 69, 72; Lesser on, 65; Trilling on, 49–50
Aesthetic response, 72, 107–109
Aesthetics of reception (Rezeptionsästhetik), 38, 85, 109–16
"Affective Fallacy, The" (Wimsatt and Beardsley), 69, 87, 90
Anatomy of Criticism (Frye), 97
Anna O., 27–28
Anthropology: on catharsis, 129n.2
Antigone (Anouilh), 58, 130n.13
Anxiety, 19, 65, 66–67, 102, 132n.11
Apollonian: in Nietzsche, 4–5
Aristotle, 38, 59, 61, 104; on catharsis, as critically interpreted, 27, 40–41, 42, 52, 54–55, 63, 84, 85–86, 110; on learning, 11, 22; on poetry, 69, 70; *Politics*, 14–15, 20; *Rhetoric*, 74; on tragedy, 49, 72, 73–74. *See also Poetics*
Arnold, Matthew, 71, 104
Art, 3, 40, 88, 98, 129n.4; Burke on, 58, 60, 62; contextualist critics on, 92–93, 95–96; ego psychologists on, 53–55; Freud on, 33–36, 45, 48, 137n.1. *See also* Imaginative literature
Artist, 36, 45–48, 56, 137n.1. *See also* Author
Associative identification, 113, 115
Audience, 8–9, 46, 58, 100–101, 116, 130n.12, 130n.13; and counter-transference, 38; Freud on, 45, 137n.1; and identification, 54–57, 74; in psychodrama, 41, 136n.47; Rabinowitz on, 144n.32; and role reversal, 63–65; and tragedy, 18, 49–52, 74. *See also* Reader; Spectator
Author, 45, 50–51, 68–70, 82–83, 85, 105–106
Author-catharsis (writer-catharsis), 19, 42, 47, 69, 130n.14; Eliot on, 78–79, 80

Auxiliary ego, 40, 136n.47
Averroes: Arabic version of *Poetics*, 131n.3

Barthes, Roland, 142n.2
Beardsley, Monroe C., 69
Beauty, 73, 75, 99–100
Benne, K. D., 42
Bernays, Jakob, 28, 117–18, 134n.2; on catharsis, 16–17, 27, 33
Beyond the Pleasure Principle (Freud), 31, 35–36, 49
Biography, 46–47
Birth of Tragedy from the Spirit of Man, The (Nietzsche), 4–5
Blackmur, R. P., 79, 82, 142n.74
Breuer, Joseph, 27–29
Brill, A. A., 29–30, 38–39
Brooks, Cleanth, 82, 83, 87–88, 94, 142n.68
Burke, Kenneth, 46, 47–48, 57–63, 83, 130n.13, 138n.16
Byron: on poet's catharsis, 19
Bywater, Ingram, 17, 132n.15

Cassirer, Ernst, 5–7
Catharsis: in aesthetics, *see* individual authors and schools of thought; in group psychotherapy, 39; in medicine, 14, 15–17
Cathartic identification (in Jauss), 112, 114, 115
Cathartic treatment (in psychoanalysis), 27–30, 32–33, 35; Ferenczi on, 37–38
Charcot, Jean Martin, 28
Christianity: and catharsis, 59–60
Cinthio, Giraldi, 18
Clarification: catharsis as, 3, 13, 22
Cleansing: Burke on, 61–62
Cognition. *See* Intellectual understanding
Coleridge, Samuel T., 64–65
Collective response: and catharsis, 58–59, 130n.14
Comedy: and catharsis, 7, 114
Communication, 3–4, 60, 62, 108, 110–11, 115–16
Conflict, 34–35, 67, 106–107
Consumption: of works of art, 109
Content, 66–67
Context, 88, 93, 94